Something's Wrong
Somewhere

Something's Wrong Somewhere

Globalization, Community and the
Moral Economy of the Farm Crisis

Christopher Lind

Fernwood Publishing
Halifax

Editing: Brenda Conroy
Design and layout: Beverley Rach
Cover Photo: Beverley Rach
Printed and bound in Canada by: Hignell Printing Limited.
A publication of:
Fernwood Publishing
Box 9409, Station A
Halifax, Nova Scotia
B3K 5S3
Second Printing, June 1996
Fernwood Publishing Company Limited gratefully acknowledges the financial support of The Ministry of Canadian Heritage.

Canadian Cataloguing in Publication Data

Lind, Christopher, 1953-

     Something's wrong somewhere
     Includes bibliographical references.

     ISBN 1-895686-49-0

1. Agriculture -- Economic aspects -- Saskatchewan.
2. Agriculture -- Environmental aspects --
Saskatchewan. 3. Saskatchewan -- Rural conditions.
I. Title.

HD1790.S37L56 1995   338.1'097124   C95-950036-7

for Sandy, who knew personally the economic cost
of an ethical life
and
for Ralph, who taught me what it meant
to be called to a place to teach

About the Cover

This elevator stands at NW 15-3-1 E, a half mile east of the Prime Meridian, the line from which all surveys of Western Canada are based.

It was built in the days of horses and wagons, when elevators were close enough so any farmer could get two loads a day into the elevator. Normally 6 miles separated them. It is the typical crib structure unique to Western Canada, which means planks are stacked to make the walls of the bins.

It was closed in the early 60s as part of a rationalization that is still going on.

Contents

Figures

ACKNOWLEDGEMENTS

This book represents the intersection of different pathways in my life. It is the response to my first economics professor who looked at me quizzically over twenty years ago when I said the value I was worried about in society was not the same as the value he was worried about in the economy. Secondly, it is another example of the contextual method in theology that I became concerned about in the late 1970s. Thirdly, it represents an application of the theoretical framework in ethics and economics I began learning and fashioning over fifteen years ago.

Finally, this book represents a landmark on another path. In 1985 I was called from urban, Anglican southern Ontario to serve as Professor of Church and Society at a United Church theological school preparing people for leadership in rural western Canada. On more than one occasion I wondered what it was, besides teaching, I was called here to do. Only after bringing this manuscript to completion did I realize this was what I was brought here to do.

Many people have accompanied me along these sometimes meandering streams. Abraham Rotstein of Massey College generously welcomed me as an ally, nurtured my understanding of the material world and eventually introduced me to the work of his friend and mentor Karl Polanyi. Gregory Baum, then of St. Michael's College, accepted me as another in a long line of students anxious to know his secrets. His affirmation of the interdisciplinary approach to theological work has been important to my own development.

Roger Hutchinson of Emmanuel College introduced me to contemporary social ethics and expanded my understanding of the Canadian Social Gospel. From him I learned that no matter how abstract a theory becomes, if it accurately describes the experience of the people, it will be understood. In Saskatchewan, it wasn't until the late Jake Bendel placed a copy of one of my academic papers on a resource table at a farm crisis workshop that I knew what Roger meant. For hundreds of farm activists on the prairie, Paul Brassard has been the glue holding the network together. My thanks to Paul for his support and to the Roman Catholic Church in Saskatchewan for enabling Paul to enable us.

Something's Wrong Somewhere

The late Eric Smith of the Saskatchewan Research Council was a great help when I was having trouble distinguishing the forest from the trees. Lee Davis Creal of Lucinda Vardey Agencies affirmed for me the importance of this work. I am grateful to Lee for her advice on the Canadian publishing industry which is suffering from globalization just like farming. I am also grateful to my brother Robin Lind who picked me up when I was down and showed me that I always have choices. The team at Fernwood Publishing, Errol Sharpe, Beverley Rach and Brenda Conroy, are also to be congratulated. Their commitment to Canadian publishing as a cultural and political act is a model for others to follow. Thank you.

I would be remiss if I did not acknowledge the support of the Academic Committee and the Board of Regents of St. Andrews College. The basic research for this book took place during a sabbatical year made possible by these two groups. The value of sabbaticals is not always apparent to people who are not involved in academic affairs on a daily basis. It requires faith in the value of intellectual work as a long term enterprise undertaken on behalf of a whole community. Though the ideas and commitments expressed here are mine alone, I hope the Regents see their interests expressed in this effort.

When the interviews were fresh and the implications newly arrived at I had the opportunity to test some ideas with a variety of audiences. My thanks go to the Faculty of Religious Studies at McGill University, the Theological School at Queen's University, Emmanuel College in Toronto, Huron College in London, the Faculties of Business and of Religious Studies at the University of Windsor and the Anglican Diocese of Calgary. The ideas present in several chapters were presented in draft form at a number of conferences. Among these were the third Karl Polanyi Conference in Milan, the annual meeting of the Canadian Society for the Study of Practical Ethics in Charlottetown, a conference on Canadian Agriculture Law in Saskatoon, the annual meeting of the Canadian Theological Society in Ottawa and a conference on Agricultural Work and Technological Change in Regina. My thanks are also due to Professor Wilfred Denis of St. Thomas College and Dr. William Crosby of the Plant Biotechnology Institute, National Research Council, for their comments on earlier drafts of what ended up as chapter three of this volume.

Most of the interview subjects were members of the Concerned Farmers of Saskatchewan, the Saskatchewan Women's Agricultural Network or the National Farmers Union. I have not named you individually because I said that I wouldn't. Nevertheless, I remain in your debt. Hopefully, my thanks will be expressed not merely by these words but by your recognition that your voices have been heard and faithfully represented in these pages.

Christopher Lind

INTRODUCTION

An Overview of the Farm Crisis in Saskatchewan

Agriculture in Saskatchewan

People who are unfamiliar with agriculture in Western Canada may wonder why we should be concerned with farming in that wide, flat Canadian province north of the North Dakota border. I think we can best understand the effects of "globalization," not by trying to grasp the whole picture at once but rather by confining our attention to one discrete frame of reference. The general issues will be revealed in the particular. The particular issue we will study here is the farm crisis in Saskatchewan.

Agriculture in Saskatchewan is not an insignificant enterprise. There is more farm land in Saskatchewan that in any other Canadian province.[1] Even though more than one-third of all Canada's class one agricultural land can be seen from the top of Toronto's CN Tower, Saskatchewan has the largest area planted to principal field crops.[2] As Figure 1 shows,[3] Saskatchewan farmers receive almost one-quarter of all farm income in Canada and hold almost one-quarter of all farm debt.[4]

One of the reasons for these figures is the significant role played by wheat and other grains in the Canadian economy. Wheat is grown in 43 percent of all Canada's crop land. In 1990, Canada produced 31.7 million tons of wheat, of which 55 percent came from Saskatchewan[5] (see Figure 2).

Wheat is not the only crop that Saskatchewan grows in abundance. The flat prairie grassland is good for growing a limited range of crops in enormous quantities. As Figure 3 shows, Saskatchewan and the other Prairie provinces dominate Canada's production of rye as well.[6] Charts could be drawn for canola, flax, mustard and the other staples of Prairie agriculture which would show similar results.

Figure 1
Significance of Saskatchewan Agriculture for Canada

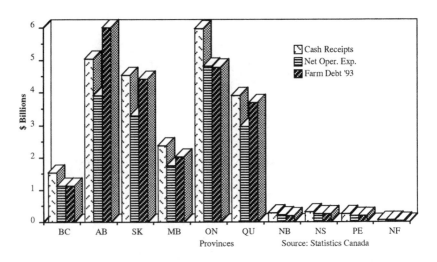

Figure 2
Wheat Production by Province

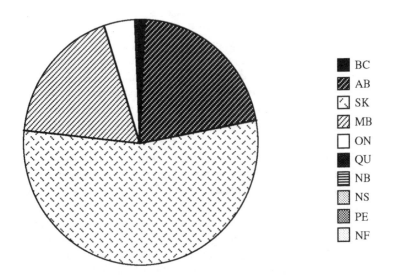

Figure 3
Rye Production by Province

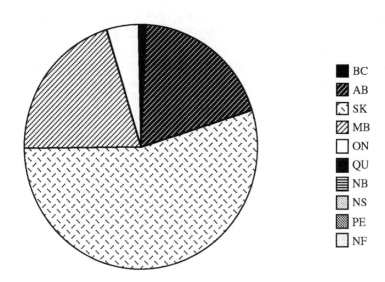

BC
AB
SK
MB
ON
QU
NB
NS
PE
NF

What is the farm crisis?

One way to describe the crisis on Saskatchewan farms is by telling a statistical story. Saskatchewan is known as an exporter of wheat and people. Having reached a peak of one million residents in the mid-1980s, a figure reached once before almost half a century earlier, Saskatchewan has been losing approximately ten thousand people per year for the last five years. This is partly due to the rural depopulation which results from the increase in farm size that occurs when industrial processes are applied to agriculture and which has continued unabated since the end of the Second World War. This depopulation does not just result in urban growth within the same province. When a poor provincial economy is matched by booming economies in other provinces, the provincial migration statistics reflect the change. The late 1980s were just such a time; the young people of Saskatchewan were leaving to make their futures in southern Ontario and the lower mainland of British Columbia.

The application of industrial processes to agriculture has also produced enormous gains in food produced. For example, in 1986, Canada produced its largest grain crop in history. But this was followed in Saskatchewan by a plague of grasshoppers and two years of severe drought. Because of the vagaries of nature, Saskatchewan farmers are always looking ahead to next year for a solution. They proudly refer to the region as "next year country " Sure enough, the second and third largest grain harvests in history were taken off in 1990 and 1991. This should have solved the problem. Unfortunately, farmers discovered they were even worse off now than they were before. Figure 4 describes the resulting despair in economic terms. Since 1983, Saskatchewan farmers have owed between $4 and $6 billion, depending on the year. Given the current relationship between income and expenses, these farmers don't have a hope of paying off the debts. The apparent fall in debts since their peak in 1986 is due partly to the large number of bankruptcies during this period (see Figure 5). From 1986 through 1993, the average value of farm land and buildings in Saskatchewan fell by 33 percent.

Figure 4
Increase in Debt on Saskatchewan Farms

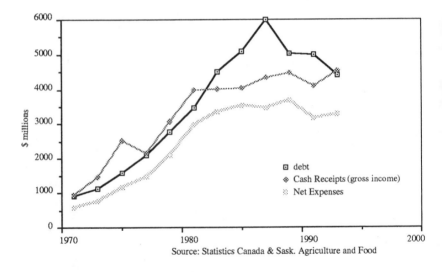

Source: Statistics Canada & Sask. Agriculture and Food

The Income Crisis

One aspect of the farm crisis is the income crisis. Figure 6 shows the average price per bushel received for Saskatchewan wheat over the last seventy-eight years.[7] The Consumer Price Index has been used to factor out the impact of inflation.[8] Prior to the late 1980s, the lowest recorded price paid for Saskatchewan wheat was in 1931 when farmers received the 1986 equivalent of $3.01 per bushel. The 1991/92 crop year price of $3.08 per bushel is equivalent to a 1986 price of approximately $2.44. That means that, in 1991, Saskatchewan farmers received a price for their wheat which was the lowest in Canadian history and approximately 19 percent lower than they received during the Great Depression. Figure 6 shows what farmers already know. There is a striking parallel between

Figure 5
Farm Bankruptcies in Saskatchewan 1979—1993

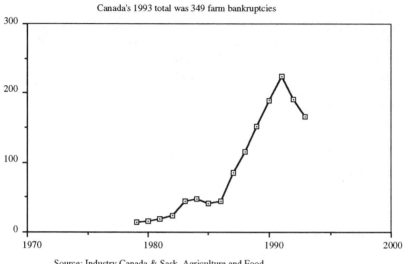

Canada's 1993 total was 349 farm bankruptcies

Source: Industry Canada & Sask. Agriculture and Food

Figure 6
History of Saskatchewan Wheat Prices 1915—1993

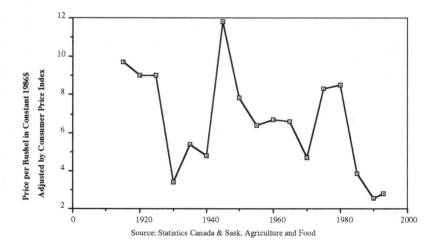

Source: Statistics Canada & Sask. Agriculture and Food

conditions now and conditions in the 1930s. There's also a tragic difference. Prices are even worse now than they were then. In 1994, Saskatchewan farmers would need a farm gate price of over $4/bushel to surpass in buying power what they received for wheat in 1931.

Figure 7 gives us a closer look at wheat prices over the last two decades. This shows exactly why Saskatchewan farmers could be so optimistic in the late 1970s and early 1980s. For a twelve year period from 1972 to 1984, the price of wheat never fell below the equivalent of $5 per bushel (in 1986 dollars). In 1973 it hit a high of $13 a bushel and spent several years around $8 a bushel half a dozen years later. Who would have guessed that after returning to a fifteen year low in 1985, it would fall completely out of bed?

The International Trade War
One of the reasons for this income crisis is the trade war between Europe and the United States. The United States is the world's largest wheat exporter with 35-40 percent of the world wheat market. The European Community (E.C.) has become the second largest exporter of wheat with over 20 percent of the world market. Canada, with almost 20 percent of the world market, is the third largest exporter. Figure 8 demonstrates the relationship between the U.S. market share

Figure 7
Saskatchewan Wheat Prices 1970—1993

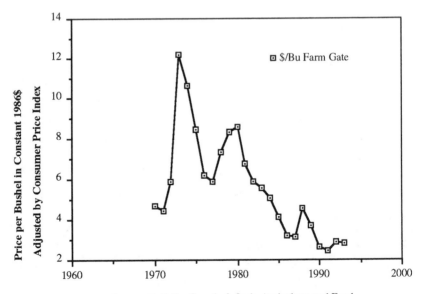

Source: Statistics Canada & Sask. Agriculture and Food

and the E.C. market share. When the E.C. share of the world market increases, the U.S. share decreases, and vice versa. This bid for market share occurs through price competition—wheat is sold below the cost paid to the domestic producer. The European Community countries operate under what is known as the Common Agricultural Program (CAP). This program is designed to provide domestic food security for E.C. countries as well as a secure economic base for their rural areas. The program has lead to overproduction of a whole range of foodstuffs, not just wheat. In order to clear this oversupply, the E.C. has been selling their wheat on the international market at whatever price they could get. This has produced a downward effect on the world price while increasing the EC's market share.

The United States, on the other hand, have had policies in place that allow for the government to purchase excess supplies of grain and then pay farmers to store it on their farms. This was a good deal for farmers but did nothing to curtail what was obviously a problem of oversupply. In 1985, at a time of declining market share, the U.S. government introduced the Export Enhancement Program (EEP). This allowed the U.S. grain-trading companies like Cargill to bid for "bonus bushels" from government stocks. These "bonus bushels" were to be used as an incentive to increase the sale of U.S. commodities to certain countries, for

Figure 8
Market Share of World Wheat and Flour Trade

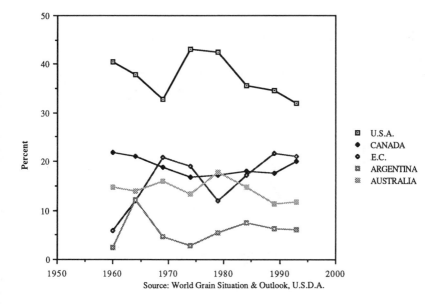

Source: World Grain Situation & Outlook, U.S.D.A.

17

example China and the former Soviet Union (but not Japan or Korea). The net effect of this program was to further depress the world price of wheat while halting the slide of the U.S. market share.

While the United States exports almost twice as much wheat as Canada does, Canada exports 75 percent of what it produces. This is a much larger percentage than any of its competitors. The U.S., by comparison, exports only 50 percent of its annual production.[9] This means that Canada is much more vulnerable to international economic forces than other participants in this market. In addition, the Canadian treasury simply doesn't have deep enough pockets to subsidize exports prices to compete with the U.S. and the E.C. When the two largest exporters are prepared to subsidize the export price to whatever level it takes to gain market share, the long term price of wheat will be not $2 per bushel but $0 per bushel.

The Expense Crisis

The expense crisis takes many forms. One of these is the high cost of borrowed money. As farmers moved from a pattern of subsistence agriculture to industrial agriculture, they expanded their land holdings, replaced manual labour with mechanical labour through the purchase of expensive, specialized equipment, and increased their productive potential through the use of high cost inputs like fertilizer, pesticides and herbicides. All of these changes mean that capital (money) plays a much larger role in prairie agriculture than it used to. Much of this money is borrowed and, in the last twenty years, Saskatchewan farmers (like all borrowers) have experienced a crisis in the cost of money.

Figure 9
Interest Paid by Saskatchewan Farmers 1971—1993

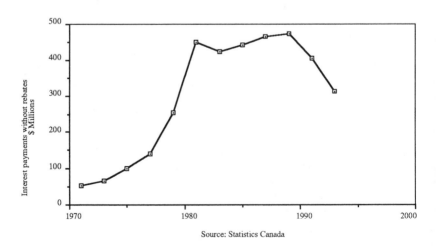

Source: Statistics Canada

18

Introduction

In 1979, interest rates started to get out of hand. They approached 20 percent in the early 1980s and they remained high throughout the decade (see Figure 9). As Figure 4 showed, the early and mid-1970s were a time of rising real income for farmers. It was also a time of rising farm land prices as farmers competed for the right to expand their operations and profit from the efficiencies promised by the federal government and other agricultural experts. This mood of optimism coupled with high land prices created some of the necessary conditions for the accumulation of debt.

The Increase in Chemical Use

The new money available to farmers was not only used to bid up the price of land. It was also used to finance the purchase of new equipment and to finance an annual increase in the application of farm chemicals (fertilizers, pesticides, and herbicides). The assumption was that these would increase production sufficiently to more than compensate for the increased costs. As Figure 10 shows, the increase in chemical use over the last twenty years has been dramatic. When you put this change together with the high cost of borrowed money, it is possible to see just how radically agriculture has changed for this generation of farmers. The cost of chemicals and the cost of borrowed money now account for almost 30 percent of net farm expenses (see Figure 11).

Figure 10
Chemical Use on Saskatchewan Farms 1971—1995

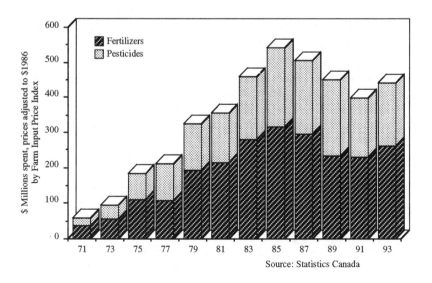

Source: Statistics Canada

Figure 11
Farm Chemicals and Interest Payments 1971—1993

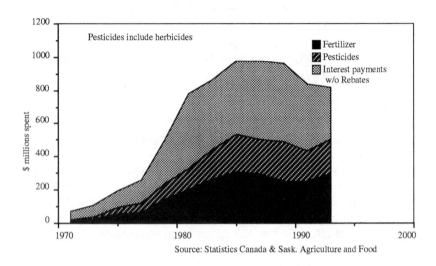

Source: Statistics Canada & Sask. Agriculture and Food

Farm Bankruptcy

Farmers in Saskatchewan who have debt problems find themselves faced with both provincial and federal debt review legislation. The province operates a Farm Land Security Board. A secured creditor who wants to foreclose on a farmer must notify both the farmer and the Board. This triggers a mandatory mediation process over a minimum of 105 days. Federal legislation has established a Farm Debt Review Board. Under this legislation, a secured creditor's attempt to seize property triggers a fifteen-day grace period during which the farmer may voluntarily apply for a review by the Board.

There are roughly 300 rural municipalities (R.M.s) in the province with an average of 200 farmers in each R.M. By July 1989 there were seventeen R.M.s where more than 20 percent of the farmers had gone through the farm debt review process at either the provincial or federal level and seventy R.M.s where less than 5 percent of the farmers had gone through the process.

Less than two years later, there were only eight R.M.s where less than 5 percent of the farmers had been through the farm debt review process and 87 R.M.s where 20 percent or more of the farmers had gone through it.

More recent data shows how rapidly the crisis has spread. Just six months later, in September 1991, there were only six R.M.s where less than 5 percent of the farmers have had their debt reviewed by government agencies. There were 120 R.M.s where more than 20 percent of the farmers had gone before the review boards and 33 R.M.s where more than 30 percent of the farmers had. By January

1993 there was no part of Saskatchewan that had escaped this trauma. There are now several R.M.s where over 50 percent of the farmers have appeared before one of the debt review boards.

Not all farmers facing insolvency go through this process. Some make their own arrangements with their creditors. Similarly, not all farmers who go through the farm debt review boards lose their land. According to 1991 figures, of the 73 percent of farmers for whom data is available 43 percent had their debt restructured or rescheduled, 43 percent quit their claim to the land and then leased it back from the lender and 7 percent had some of their assets sold.[10]

It should come as no surprise, given the extent of the crisis on Saskatchewan farms and the speed with which it has spread, that there is a human cost which appears in the form of farm suicides, drug abuse, alcoholism, family breakdown and domestic violence. The present pattern is unsustainable. One credit union executive predicted that if it doesn't change, in five years the population of the province will be cut in half to 500,000 people.

How should we evaluate this crisis from a moral point of view?

If we want to evaluate this crisis from an ethical perspective, we need to be careful to avoid turning to someone schooled in the conventions of formal economics. These conventions require that most of the moral content be emptied from the economic vessels in our larder. All that will remain will be the tantalizing vapours of contract—a concern for fair dealing, legal obligation, and efficiency.

From the perspective of formal economics, it is both natural and proper that humans should be primarily motivated by their material self-interests. It is assumed that the resources to satisfy these material interests are in short supply. Formal economists work from the starting point that the market mechanism is the most efficient mechanism for adjudicating the competition between too many material self-interests and not enough resources. From this point of view, the moral dimension of the farm crisis can be reduced to just one facet—a question about the efficiency of agricultural markets.

This is not how most people approach moral questions in their lives, even ones with a significant economic component. Because formal economics obscures from view most moral concern, one way to reclaim it is by taking the perspective of those protesting economic change. When people protest economic change and say something is wrong, they have in mind at least some idea of what is right. I have attempted to reclaim this moral dimension by interviewing farmers involved in farm protest in Saskatchewan. In chapter two I explain the theoretical background for this approach, based on the historian, E.P. Thompson, and the economic theorist, Karl Polanyi. In that chapter I also describe the scene in Rosetown, Saskatchewan, in October 1991 when farmers came together in what was to that point the largest farm rally in the province's history.[11] As one farmer put it:

I may not know as much about the world market as some of those professionals out there, but what I do know is that it's wrong. It's all wrong and we've got to change it.

In total, fifteen farmers were interviewed during the course of eleven different interviews. All of the interviews took place between the late fall of 1991 and the early summer of 1992. The first interviewees were prominently involved in the Rosetown Rally of October 1991. Others were referred to me by the people I originally interviewed. Many of the interview subjects would associate themselves with a loose grouping of farmers known as the Concerned Farmers of Saskatchewan. Some of the them would associate themselves with the National Farmers Union (NFU), others with the Saskatchewan Women's Agricultural Network (SWAN). At least one person was not formally associated with any of these organisations.

Farm Rally or Farm Protest?

All of the farmers interviewed were involved in what I term "farm protest" of one kind or another in 1991/92. Most attended the Rosetown Rally. Not all of the farmers interviewed were comfortable with the term "protest" to describe their actions. In general, those not associated with the NFU were the most uncomfortable.

I hate the word protest. I have never considered what we have done to be a protest. I think there it is a constructive way of bringing farmers together in a totally non-militant way. To provide solutions to the situation we are in.

We even had a hard time, we even discussed using the word rally. We thought, [maybe] just the word meeting. They thought they would put a little more oompf into it.

Our media right after the Rosetown Rally kept saying 4,000 angry farmers showed up. They were not really angry. They were just voicing their opinion really. When you hear the word angry you always think of big riots or something like that. Which it wasn't. It was kept in order and people never yelled or shouted profanities. They basically spoke their peace of mind. They were frustrated, but that's about it. Everyone is frustrated at times.

To me I would never say protest. I would say more rally. . . . Protest is like people using violence and they are hitting each other with clubs— to me that is a protest. So this was more like a rally, like a meeting.

People came out and voiced their opinions. There was not violence or anything.

When you think of protest you think radical. You don't think of rational people.

I tend to take a soft line on what this whole protest movement is about. The word almost comes a little more hard than I see it. It is, obviously, and yet in my mind not in an antagonistic sort of sense. Our group have tried to be fairly moderate, tried to be non-partisan. We've tried to work with the people we're trying to talk to rather than try and confront them in any way that's going to alienate them.

We are all just average farmers. . . . We are going to chair the meeting ourselves and we are not going to dress up. We are going to wear average decent clothes. We don't want any airs. And that is why we did not bring in any special speakers. We would have brought in economists. People talking numbers. No. We just had farmers talking over their viewpoints.

To stand up and talk in front of four thousand people is not my place. I have enough trouble talking in front of twenty local farmers at a meeting or a service club meeting or whatever. If the situation arose, stand up and fight for what you want to survive. It is different. I don't know if I would have volunteered to have been part of the Rosetown Rally, but I guess I was part of the starting crew, so I could not back down. You get into something and you can't get out of it. I am very glad that I went through with it.

I just look around town and I see how tough times are, with all the houses vacant, people leaving friends that you knew and grew up with and all of a sudden, they are gone trying to make a go of it elsewhere, people going bankrupt. [This] generally has been a pretty prosperous area. The oil from the West and the farming. Now when you see people going like that it scares me. That is why I am involved now. Number one it is trying to help out and number two you're scared. [You're scared?] Yah, where the hell is this thing going to go?

The Oxford English Dictionary describes a rally as something that might take place after a conflict, as when an army "rallies" after having retreated. Yet the resistance to the idea of protest and the attachment to the alternative word, rally, seemed to be about something other than dictionary definitions. Clearly, the event at Rosetown was a rally—farmers were reassembled after having been dispersed. It was just as clearly a protest since it gave formal expression to dissent and disapproval. The significance of the words has to do with distance.

On the one hand, the organisers of the Rosetown Rally wanted to distance themselves from the National Farmers Union. To them, the NFU was associated with visible political dissent and sometimes even with civil disobedience. On the other hand, the organizers did not want to distance themselves from people in authority. They spoke often of the need to conduct their affairs "in a professional manner." They also spoke of the need to approach their problems "in a rational way." They worked on the assumption that if the politicians in Ottawa and in Regina understood the facts of the case, they would take action to rectify the situation. This attitude was not shared by all whom I interviewed but it was the dominant view of the organizers of the rally.

After much deliberation, I have decided to continue to use the term "farm protest" to describe what I witnessed. I think of this word in historical terms as will become apparent in chapter two. Readers should keep in mind, however, that a significant number of my interview subjects would prefer a less contentious word.

In the interviews, I listened with the ears of an ethicist. I wanted to discover, not the economic analyses (which were diverse), but the "moral" categories used by farmers involved in what I was terming farm protest. Four moral categories or themes emerged from those conversations. They are: 1) the significance of agriculture for national sovereignty; 2) the need for cooperation amid the loss of community; 3) the crisis in the family who farms; and 4) an increasing sense of powerlessness. As I discuss in chapter four, all of these categories have to do with different aspects of community. The nation is the largest unit of community and the family is the smallest.

The Four Moral Categories

1) The significance of agriculture for national sovereignty

In chapter one, I describe being surprised when the rally started with the singing of our national anthem, O Canada. When I saw a farmer carrying a homemade placard saying, "Break the farmer, break the nation," I knew there was a larger issue here. From the farmers' point of view, if the government saves the Canadian farmer from destruction, it would be saving Francophone farmers and Anglophone farmers, Western farmers and Eastern farmers, young farmers and old farmers, male farmers and female farmers. It would be rescuing a population group that cuts across all the major divisions in contemporary society. These farmers were not just making a regional pitch. As one of them said, "We're not Saskatchewan farmers, we're Canada's farmers."

There was also a more subtle and more profound issue here. This became more apparent in detailed follow-up interviews. The farmers were saying that there was a difference between food production and other kinds of production.

Introduction

They were saying there was a connection between a country having a viable domestic food supply and its ability to conduct its affairs without external threats or interference. "If rural Saskatchewan isn't there then rural Alberta and rural Manitoba won't be there either. Nor will a good part of rural Ontario be there," another farmer pointed out. "Now you've lost the food supply of your nation. You've got to go south to the U.S. for your food. Then you'll have to pay for it!" These farmers had a serious concern about their country's sovereignty and a claim that their own contribution to that future was being ignored. "A sound agricultural base will make things better across the nation," some of them said. "Pay the farmer and all of Canada prospers."

2) The need for cooperation and community

Another theme that was sounded on numerous occasions was both a self criticism and a call to action. Farm people were concerned about the eroding base of their communities. They recognized that they had failed to work together in the past and they called on each other to show the level of cooperation that would be required to survive. "We need to get together or we'll all be gone," they said to one another. "By ourselves we are all dust." They acknowledged that there were forces that were driving them apart and that private (self) interest had triumphed in the past. "We need to work together and cooperate for the common good." This claim was widely applauded at the Rosetown Rally. "We can have an impact because we came here together today," they said.

A strong connection was being made between the sustainability of farm families and the sustainability of rural communities. "Tell the people that they're going to have to start supporting the family farm. Make sure you put *family* farm in there. We don't want corporate farms. Co-ops are okay but we don't want huge corporations in here. Let the families stay out there. We want the community to stay there." The theme of community was obviously connected in an intimate way with the crisis facing farm families.

3) The crisis in the family who farms

For some years, I have heard people talk about and identify the crisis on the family farm. The emphasis has always been on the noun "farm" modified by the adjective "family," as in, "Look what's happening to the farm operation run by families." Now people were emphasising the noun "family" modified by the adverb "farm," as in, "Look what's happening to the family who farms." This idea is expressed in many different ways. Sometimes it has an economic dimension as in, "The average grain farmer is living well below the poverty line." Sometimes it has a generational dimension as in, "You don't see many young farmers here because there aren't any left"; and "I'm twenty years old. There are young people out there who want to farm"; and "We want our kids around and feeling good about farming thirty years from now." On other occasions it

25

suggests a darker side to farm life. "We're tired of seeing our husbands grow old before their time," said one woman. "We lash out at those nearest—our families," said a man.

For some farmers, the crisis is forcing them into a pattern of relationships that they wouldn't choose under different conditions. "It's a shame that both parents must work," said one farmer, "when one would rather stay home and look after our nation's most precious resource—children." Through all the comments, like a dulcimer's drone, one can also hear wounded pride and diminished self worth. As one woman put it, "I'm a third-generation farm wife and mother and damn proud of it." All of the farmers I talked to would agree that they're not fighting to maintain just any kind of farming but agriculture of a particular sort. "You want to fight for the future of our *family* farms." The crisis has now become a crisis in the most intimate of communities—the family.

4) An increasing sense of powerlessness

The desire to protest is motivated by the need to change circumstances, but underlying the protest is a claim about power and who is really in control. Saskatchewan farmers know that their wheat is highly prized the world over for its high gluten content. It's often added to other flours in order to make them "harder" and therefore better for bread making. This knowledge makes their sense of powerlessness more difficult to bear. "We are forced to accept $2 per bushel for the best damn wheat in the world," they said. Some farmers, like the government, interpret the crisis as arising primarily out of the international trade war. Their moral outrage is almost visceral. "What these countries are doing to us," they say, "is internationally immoral and an abomination on world trade." "Stop this debilitating madness and start trading fairly."

Others identify that, although farmers are not alone in the agricultural process, they seem to be at the end of the line when it comes to having any influence on events. "What protection does the farmer have?" they ask. "What protection does the bank have?" Still others feel the indifference of a society that wants to hold farmers individually at fault. "We feel the blame that others seem to be putting on us."

The sense of powerlessness seems so real and so deep that many farmers feel they are the ones who are being farmed. "The farmer and his wife are now expected to work off the farm to support the farming habit," said one. "The system is farming the farmers," said another. Some farmers are using even more powerful metaphors. "Fifty percent of the farm population is farmer wives. Our labour is slave labour," said one woman. "Farm labour is slave labour," said another in agreement. Echoing a complaint as old as Moses, another said, "We can no longer work like slaves and work more and more for less and less." The sense of powerlessness was aggravated by the realization that their primary activity was no small matter in the larger scheme of things. "The most important thing is growing food."

Introduction

After identifying these moral categories, I then returned to the formal economic data. I asked, "What interpretation of this data is consistent with the moral categories used by the farmers themselves?" Chapter one follows the moral concern for agricultural sovereignty. It traces that deep anxiety among farmers to a revolution in international finance called "globalization." By telling the story of this revolution, it also helps explain where this extraordinary farm debt comes from—the same place third world debt comes from. It comes not from poor management but from the integration of national capital markets. One of its consequences is to erode the power of national governments over monetary forces. This chapter moves from a consideration of economic history to the ethics of globalization. It contrasts the new ethic of competitiveness, domination and indifference with a religious ethic of cooperation, solidarity and compassion.

Chapter two begins by telling the story of the Rosetown rally. It goes on to provide the theoretical justification for the concept of moral economy and to discuss how ethics became separated from economics in our everyday understanding.

Chapter three takes up the expense crisis in the contexts of environmental degradation, powerlessness and community. It suggests that community needs to be rebuilt in a way that includes the community of the land. It draws parallels between the ethics of globalization and the ethics of industrialized agriculture. It suggests that agriculture needs to be re-modelled, based on an ethic of friendship not domination. Chapter four considers what responses might be available to us and proposes intentionally building community as a response to globalization. It begins with a story about rural dignity. It goes on to consider what we mean by the term community, and distinguishes it from association and civil society. The chapter also analyzes the mechanism by which globalization erodes community and proposes a new mechanism by which that process can be reversed. It suggests a practical way to build community with and among farmers who are losing their land. At the conclusion of the book the lessons of globalization and community are summarized in the form of a modern parable about farm life entitled, "The Parable of the Fences."

Notes

1. Saskatchewan contains 65.7 million acres, which is almost 40 percent of Canada's total of 167.6 million acres. Source: Statistics Canada, 1986 data.
2. Saskatchewan has 31.5 million acres planted to principal field crops out of a Canadian total of 79 million acres. Source: Statistics Canada, 1990 data.
3. All charts have been prepared by the author unless otherwise noted.
4. 1993 Canadian realized net farm income was $2.8 billion. Saskatchewan farmers received $513.9 million. 1993 Canadian farm debt outstanding as of December 1 was $22.7 billion. Saskatchewan farmers owed $4.4 billion of that. Alberta farmers owed $5.99 billion.

5. Saskatchewan produced 17.3 million tonnes in 1990. Source: Statistics Canada.

6 In 1990, Canada produced 939,000 tonnes of wheat. Of that total, Saskatchewan produced 513,000 tonnes, Manitoba 193,000 tonnes and Alberta 181,000 tonnes, Source: Statistics Canada, *Farming Facts 1991*, Catalogue 21-522E.

7. The data has been collected according to crop years so that the price reported for 1940, for example, is the price received for the 1940/41 crop year.

8. The Consumer Price Index (CPI) from the first half of the year has been used. For example, the nominal price received for the 1940/41 crop year has been adjusted by the average CPI for 1940.

9. In 1988/89 the U.S.A. exported 46.2 percent of its production. In 1989/90 the U.S.A. exported 51.3 percent of its production. Source: USDA *World Grain Situation and Outlook*, FG 10-91.

10. Farm Debt Review Board, Regina, Sask. September 1991.

11. In January 1992 it was superceded by a rally at SaskPlace in Saskatoon when 13,000 farmers and their allies came together at an event sponsored by the Saskatchewan Wheat Pool.

CHAPTER ONE

Agricultural Sovereignty, Farm Debt and the Ethics of Globalization

Most of my interviews were conducted with farmers in their homes, around the kitchen table. However, not all of them could be handled that way. Sometimes, I would arrange to meet them when they came into Saskatoon. At one time or another they all did. One of my learnings from this was that a Saskatchewan farmer does more driving than a Barrie commuter.

On this occasion, Don (not his real name) had come into town to attend a meeting of school board trustees. He was sharing a room in a cinder block motel and we talked over Great Western beer and a long succession of Du Maurier Lights.

I described my project once more of interviewing farmers involved in farm protest. "Rosetown wasn't a protest," he said. "It was a rally." I recalled hearing the same thing in my first interview. A farm wife had told me that protest conjures up the image of violence. "Protest means fringe—radical," she said. "We're all just average farmers. . . . We don't want special airs." Her husband had confirmed this approach. "People think farmers are all muscles and no brains. . . . The way [the Rosetown organisers] are going about it is so professional."

Don described the phone calls he had received from British Columbia to Ontario calling for more radical action. Some people wanted to withhold grain. Others wanted to take a backhoe to the highway. Still others wanted a general strike. "I abhor that sort of thing," he said.

"I think that a reasonable man, talking to a reasonable man, Brian Mulroney or whomever, should be able to explain in a reasonable sense, and because we are right, then it will happen. You can't destroy a whole quarter of a nation because somebody wants cheap food. It doesn't make any sense. . . . If you destroy agriculture, you destroy Alberta, Saskatchewan and Manitoba."

I described my puzzlement at the singing of the national anthem at the Rosetown Rally and the handpainted sign saying, "Break the farmer—Break the nation." I asked him to explain the connection and the concern. "If rural Saskatchewan isn't there," he replied, "then rural Alberta and rural Manitoba won't be there either, nor will a good part of rural Ontario be there either. Now you've lost the food supply of your nation. You've got to go south to the U.S. for your food. Then you'll have to pay for it!"

His roommate had now joined us and opened another beer as he offered this comparison. "What's the difference between choosing to import our shoes rather than produce our own and choosing to import our food rather than produce our own?"

"You can do without a pair of shoes," he said. "You couldn't be held to ransom for a pair of shoes but you could be for food. Any nation that has lost their ability to produce food has gone under."

I began to understand. Even though Saskatchewan farmers were overwhelmingly involved in wheat farming and most of that was exported, these farmers had a perception that agriculture as such was being abandoned by their government. Their moral concern was that agriculture was not just a business like any other business. There was a fundamental connection between a country's ability to feed itself and its ability to be a nation. As we talked I began to inquire about Don's personal situation. How was the farm crisis affecting him personally?

"Until the grain sector collapsed," he replied, "we were just kind of sneaking along. Now, for the first time, we can't pay off last years operating loan. . . . It seems like everybody's getting paid but us," he said. "In three days I hauled in $50,000 worth of wheat and I lost $3000." His eyes were barely concealing his rage. His fingers were turning white around the bottle. I asked him how long he could go on like this? He lowered his face and began to cry.

"It's either fight or lose my farm and I'm not going to lose my farm without a fight." Embarrassed at this uncharacteristic display of vulnerability, he got up from the table and hurried to the bathroom. He pointed at the tape recorder. "Shut that damn thing off!"

What is globalization?

The term "globalization" is a new word that has entered our lexicon primarily by way of the business press. It has acquired a number of different meanings depending on who is using it and the context in which it is being used. In the popular business press it is often used to refer to the increased pressure on manufacturers to sell and build in more than one country. They are encouraged to think of their market, not in national terms, but in global terms. From this point of view, the North American Free Trade Agreement (NAFTA) is both a political response to globalization and an invitation to globalize.

In the popular non-business press, it can mean a new consciousness of the whole globe as a single entity. Crudely following the ideas of Marshall McLuhan, globalization means the new consciousness that we are living in a global village. It often has some media reference point. The town crier of this community is now Ted Turner's CNN Headline News which can be viewed in hotels around the globe.

In Christian circles, it can mean something else again. In 1988 the Association of Theological Schools released a report prepared by its Task Force on Globalization. For some in that group, the term meant moving missiological concerns "from the periphery to the centre of the theological enterprise" (Thomas 1989). For others it meant a new awareness that "the context for ministry and scholarship is now global" (Heim 1990).[1]

These are useful concepts but they all refer exclusively to changes in awareness or consciousness and carry with them notions of approval: an expanded awareness or consciousness is clearly a good thing to have. What they obscure is the changed material reality in people's lives and the new set of power relationships that are being played out on the newly constructed global stage. They also make it more difficult to make a different judgement about the effects of this new thing called globalization. If it's supposed to be so good, why does it hurt so much?

For these reasons I want to restrict the definition of globalization to that process which has led to the creation of a single, international (global) financial or capital market. It happened in stages over the last twenty or thirty years and its effects are nothing short of revolutionary.[2]

I think our grandchildren will look back on the end of the twentieth century and talk about these changes in the same way that we look back on the changes that ended the eighteenth century. We called those changes the Industrial Revolution.[3] The Deputy Governor of the Bank of England described the 1980s this way: "During the last two or three years . . . international banking—and indeed financial activity more generally—has embarked on changes which are probably as far-reaching as any in its long history. . . . But these will, I think, be outstripped in the breadth of their impact, both on financial institutions and on the range of instruments available to borrowers and lenders, by what is going on now" (quoted in Hamilton 1986: 13).

Where did globalization come from?
At the end of the Second World War, the international trading system needed to be rebuilt. The United States had all the money and the industrial infrastructure of Europe was in a shambles. In 1944 a conference was held at Bretton Woods, New Hampshire, to plan the post-war world. One of the participants was the English economist, John Maynard Keynes.

The financial resources of the industrial world needed to be redistributed and post-war currencies needed to be stabilized. The International Monetary Fund

(IMF) and the International Bank for Reconstruction and Development (World Bank) were established for these purposes. Although Keynes had recommended a more flexible currency system, it was agreed that most currencies (and most importantly the U.S. dollar) would be backed by gold at $35 per ounce. In 1933 President Roosevelt had changed American law to prevent American citizens from being able to redeem their dollars for gold at the bank. By contrast, Canadians of a certain age will still be able to remember going to the Bank of Nova Scotia and buying a troy ounce of gold for the equivalent of U.S.$35 up until the early 1970s. At the international level though, it was still the way national governments balanced their accounts. Governments without a large domestic supply of gold could hold American dollars instead because it was "as good as gold."

In the 1950s, as trade was being rebuilt and the Korean War was being fought, the U.S. dollar became the *de facto* international currency. Even Germans trading with Spaniards would use U.S. dollars as their medium of exchange. Through this period there grew up a pool of U.S. dollars that never got returned to the U.S. They just circulated from one international capital to another as the preferred medium of exchange. This process became known as the Eurodollar market, and in 1959 it represented about U.S.$1 billion. Transnational corporations came to rely on it more and more as an inexpensive source for borrowed money, and it grew very rapidly. As Andrew Kreiger notes, "By 1973 the sum of U.S. dollars sloshing around in the Euromarket was about $80 billion. By 1977 the Eurodollar market would amount to some $380 billion" (Krieger 1992: 127). By 1987, the Eurocurrency market (which now included new currencies, hence the new name) totalled nearly U.S.$4 trillion (Levich and Walter 1989: 53).

In the 1960s, while international lending and trade through the Eurodollar market was booming, the United States was rapidly expanding its money supply to pay for the Vietnam War. This was creating a trade imbalance because the U.S. bought more imported than domestic goods. At the end of 1970, total claims against the dollar were three times greater than the gold reserves (Kreiger 1992: 136). For some time a crisis was averted. The Federal Reserve put pressure on central banks not to demand gold and those central banks "did everything possible to avoid buying surplus dollars from the domestic banks" (Bolton 1970: 7). However, in early August 1971, when Britain inquired about redeeming U.S.$3 billion for gold, the crisis arrived. The U.S. realized that they had just been asked to produce a quarter of their gold reserves in one transaction. On August 15, 1971 President Nixon announced that the U.S. dollar would no longer be convertible to gold (Kreiger 1992: 138). Since that time, in spite of various agreements to manage currency values, most international currencies have had a floating value relative to each other.[4] Those values are now determined in a market created by daily transactions that are sometimes estimated to be in the range of U.S.$500 billion to U.S.$700 billion (Kreiger 1992: 14) but are probably much greater.

When the gold standard was abandoned, the oil producing countries (OPEC) worried that their own assets and income producing potential would be severely eroded. Their response was to put the price of oil on a "gold standard." The rapid rise in the price of oil became known to us as the "oil shock" of 1973. This produced a new in-flow of *U.S. $150 billion* into the economies of these countries *each year*—much more than they could absorb. They invested this money in U.S. and European banks. All of a sudden, the large international banks had enormous, new sources of capital to lend. It was at this time that the commercial lending policies of the banks became so aggressive. This was also the period in which most of the original Third World debt was accumulated. As Adrian Hamilton put it, "[The financial system could manage]...only because the oil producers, being relatively unsophisticated in finance, preferred to use the banks as the natural channel for their surplus funds. The first result of this 'intermediation,' as it is called, was the explosion in international banking and syndicated loans (or lending by groups of banks) of the 1970s. The subsequent debt crisis among Third World borrowers has been in the headlines ever since" (1986: 22).

A second result has been a dramatic shift away from direct foreign investment and toward international bank finance. What has emerged is an "international credit economy." "Take the case of South Korea. In 1960, direct investment accounted for 82 percent of all capital in-flow, and borrowing on the international money market only 18 percent. By 1975, the proportions had been reversed. France's 'contribution' to the industrialization of the Third World in 1976 broke down in exactly the same proportions" (Lipietz 1987: 106).

The transformation of the international financial system was still only partially understood. The forced recycling of Western consumption dollars into OPEC investment dollars into Third World debt dollars could have been positive except for the developments of 1979. In October of that year, Paul Volcker, the head of the U.S. Federal Reserve Board, decided to try and control American inflation by restricting the money supply. He did this by raising the cost of money lent to commercial banks. This would have been an unexceptional manoeuver had it been done by the Governor of the Bank of Canada, but it was done by the U.S. Federal Reserve Board. In spite of the fact that the U.S. was no longer on the gold standard, the U.S. dollar was still the world's currency. Most international trade was carried on in U.S. dollars. Most foreign governments continued to back their currencies with U.S. dollars. By raising the central bank rate in the U.S., Paul Volker was effectively raising the central bank rate for the world.[5] Prairie farmers who paid interest on their loans at 18 percent or 20 percent in 1983 can look to these events as their cause. In 1982, Mexico stopped making payments on its foreign debt for the same reason. Mexico had lost control over its own interest rates and economic policy. The debt had suddenly ballooned out of all proportion to Mexico's ability to pay.

Figure 1.1 shows how globalization affected Saskatchewan farmers. In

1971, Saskatchewan's farmers were paying $53 million a year in interest. In the mid-1970s interest payments started to increase as bankers aggressively sought to increase their lending. In 1979, the increase became dramatic and by 1981, those same farmers had increased their interest payments to almost $450 million each year. These amounts do not include any repayment of principal.

What does globalization look like?

In contrast to the despair among borrowers and the worldwide recession of 1981–1983, the financial centres were experiencing unprecedented opportunities for gain. More and more corporations and institutions were borrowing and lending outside of traditional domestic arrangements. The national capital markets of New York, London, Paris, Frankfurt, Toronto, Tokyo, and Hong Kong were now linked by computer—a North American trader could now trade twenty-four hours a day, moving from time zone to time zone. In fact, "the fastest growing exchange in the world is not an exchange in the old-fashioned sense at all. It is an electronic network of dealing on computer screens in the U.S.: NASDAQ, the National Association of Securities Dealers Automated Quotations, the third largest stock market in the world" (Hamilton 1986: 16).

This merging of markets was both caused by, and in turn precipitated, a whole new series of financial practices as well as a vast re-organisation of institutions. It used to be that corporations went to banks to borrow money, brokers to raise equity capital, and foreign exchange dealers to exchange currency. All of these separate activities took place on a national basis and were

Figure 1.1
Interest Paid by Saskatchewan Farmers 1971—1991

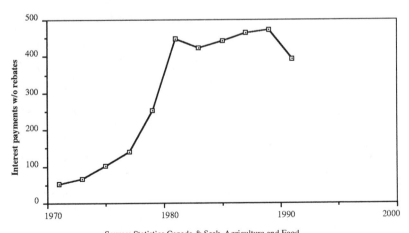

Source: Statistics Canada & Sask. Agriculture and Food

separately regulated by law and by national regulatory agencies. This is now no longer the case. Corporations can now borrow on an international market using "commercial paper" and meet their foreign exchange needs by having their own "in house" traders hedge their needs on the foreign exchange futures market. For example, when the world's biggest land developer (Olympia & York) built the office tower complex in Toronto known as First Canadian Place, they didn't finance it with a mortgage; they issued a bond which was traded on the bond market worldwide. This manoeuver has two features which are typical of the process of globalization. These features are called "disintermediation" and "securitization."

By going straight to the bond market for financing, Olympia & York were able to borrow money more cheaply. By doing so they bypassed the banks and so *dis*pensed with the usual *intermediary*, hence "disintermediation." By issuing a bond they were able to take what otherwise would have been a conventional loan and convert it into a *security* (in this case a bond) which could be bought and sold in a secondary market, hence "securitization."

The reorganisation of institutions is exemplified by the transformation of American Express. Most well known in this century for its development of the traveller's cheque into a common medium of exchange, its subsequent development of the credit card meant that it was handling vast sums of money on a daily basis. In 1981 it purchased the American brokerage house Shearson Loeb Rhoades, Inc., and in 1984, Lehman Brothers Kuhn Loeb, Inc. In the same year it purchased the British brokerage house L. Messel and more recently in Canada, it has applied for a charter as a bank.

Similarly, in Canada the Royal Bank purchased the brokerage firm Dominion Securities and the Canadian Imperial Bank of Commerce (CIBC) purchased Canada's largest brokerage house, Wood Gundy. Keeping in mind that we are still talking about the creation of a "global" market, in 1985 the Royal Bank purchased the British brokerage Kitcat & Aitken. Two months later the CIBC purchased London's Grenfell & Colegrave.[6] In 1986, England deregulated its financial markets in order to allow London to continue to be a node in this new, single, global financial market. Clearly, Canadian banks are determined to be major players in this newly globalized world.

Even though the United States renounced the gold standard in 1971 and it took over ten years for countries to realise the U.S. no longer had the power to control foreign exchange, it was clear to some that all aspects of international trade would now have a significant foreign currency aspect. Futures contracts had become big business on the Chicago Mercantile Exchange(CME) in the early 1960s with the development of the frozen pork belly contract. In the early 1970s the CME's Leo Melamed and University of Chicago economist Milton Friedman "approached the board of the First National Bank of Chicago with the idea of trading not corn or cattle, but cash . . ." (Diamond and Kollar 1989: 10). The market for financial futures was born. In 1984 the Chicago Mercantile Exchange joined with Singapore to offer twenty-four-hour-a-day trading in financial futures. "In 1987, of more than 310 million futures contracts traded throughout the world, 66 percent were traded in Chicago. . . . Currently, 350 different kinds of futures contracts can be traded" (Diamond and Kollar 1989: 13). Now, "the foreign-exchange market dwarfs the combined operations of the New York, London, Frankfurt, and Tokyo stock exchanges" (Kreiger 1992: 15).

What are the effects of globalization?

The net effect of the deregulation and integration of the international capital market(s) has been a significant erosion of the power of any single government to independently control monetary policy and an exaggeration of the differences between these same governments. Countries with foreign exchange surpluses have much greater surpluses and countries, like Canada, with foreign exchange deficits have much greater deficits (see Kuttner 1991: 232 and also Strange 1988: 8). Around the world, the response to this newly created instability and uncertainty has been the move toward regional trading blocs like the European Community and the North American Free Trade Agreement (NAFTA) involving Canada, the U.S., and Mexico. The European attempt to establish a common currency (the ECU) is an indication that such trading blocs provide powerful incentives toward a common attempt to manage the relevant currencies.

The movement toward a single, global capital market also changes the balance of power within nations. "In virtually every nation, the consequences of international financial integration has been domestic political conflict among groups with contending economic interests. It has created or reinforced sectors, firms, investors, and workers whose livelihood depends on the free movement of capital and goods across borders. But global financial integration has endangered the interests of other groups whose well-being is threatened by exposure to international competition for capital or markets" (Freiden 1987: 239).

Globalization has a paradoxical character. It seems beyond our control and yet, this global market is a human creation. Prior to the 1960s this space called the global financial market hardly existed. Yet, "by 1982 outstanding American loans to the five largest Latin American debtors—Mexico, Brazil, Argentina, Venezuela, and Chile—were larger than the total capital of the United States' entire banking system" (Freiden 1987: 119). This means that, "the ability of the contemporary international financial system to shift billions of dollars from place to place in minutes gives the markets something akin to veto power over domestic or international decisions" (Freiden 1987: 113). Even the most powerful countries can't control the price of their own currency. "The global foreign-exchange market could soak up the entire foreign-currency reserves of the ten leading industrial nations in a day's trading" (Hamilton 1989: 61).[7]

In 1989 the total daily foreign exchange volume was estimated to be

36

U.S.$650 billion. It is now thought to be well over U.S.$1 trillion. A survey conducted by the Bank of Canada in April 1992 indicated that chartered banks and other financial institutions carried out foreign exchange transactions totalling U.S.$461 billion in this country alone. This is an increase of 54 percent in three years (Bank of Canada 1992: 23-35).

On the other hand, all markets are social facts not natural facts. They are created by human action, freed up by conscious intervention, advanced by political consent. "For those concerned about broad social issues, unencumbered markets are no more an immutable given than malaria or illiteracy" (Freiden 1987: 243).

Thus the globalization of the world's financial markets leads to significant financial instability, an erosion of national power and therefore sovereignty, a defensive movement toward regional trading arrangements, and a need to reassert sovereignty at a supranational level.

The Response of Farmers

It is appropriate to remind ourselves that Canadian farmers are not the only farming group adversely affected by globalization. "Like many developing countries, American farmers borrowed heavily in the 1970s to invest in new land and machinery, for they expected a continuation of rising farm prices and of interest rates barely above the rate of inflation. After 1980, when interest rates rose and prices fell, farmers across the country had to meet doubled or tripled interest payments with shrinking sales. Between 1980 and 1986, farm prices dropped 20 percent while the cost of farming rose 15 percent. The farmers, like the debtor countries, worked harder to get by. Still, farm income dropped precipitously in the 1980s to one-half its 1970s levels as from 1980 to 1986 the number of family farmers fell by one-quarter" (Freiden 1987: 180).

The comparative figures for farmers in Saskatchewan are portrayed in Figure 1.2 which shows how rapidly farm expenses continued to climb through 1985 while net income remained flat or declined. This squeeze produced a debt which is completely unmanageable.

The devastating effects of globalization on Prairie agriculture provide us with a context in which we can interpret the moral claims of Canadian farmers protesting economic change. In the first instance, farmers are making a connection between a loss of sovereignty and the crisis in agriculture. An analysis of globalization shows us that national sovereignty is indeed under attack. The states that are being held up to us as models for the future are states with no domestic agriculture. For example, Kenichi Ohmae, in his best selling book *The Borderless World*, promotes Hong Kong and Singapore as the way of the future. He writes: "I believe the Singaporean solution is the right one, because in the global economy, economic interlinkage increases security." (Ohmae 1990: 14) He seeks to calm our fears about the future of agriculture. "The fact that primary (agricultural, forestry, fishery) industries slip out of a country and even second-ary (manufacturing) industries go overseas is not the end of the world from an employment point of view" (Ohmae 1990: 15). From the perspective of many economists and business leaders, these are small losses when weighed against the gains. The gains will result from the efficient use of capital. Even the Economic Council of Canada believes, "from the point of view of the world economy, globalization promises a better allocation of savings and investment" (Economic Council of Canada 1989: 7).

Farmers are also protesting their powerlessness and the powerlessness of their representatives. If national governments have lost significant control over the economic levers that they have traditionally relied upon to solve economic problems, then it should come as no surprise that people feel powerless in response. Their feelings are justified. They really do have less power than they used to.

Farmers are protesting the loss of community and calling on each other for more cooperation in response. Globalization is more than an event. It's a revolution. In its revolutionary phase it recalls our collective experience with the Industrial Revolution. As Karl Polanyi so insightfully analysed, the Industrial Revolution was the occasion when market society announced its full presence in the world. At that time, individual markets were linked to form a market system. Prior to that, the economic dimension of human relationships was embedded in

Figure 1.2
Income and Expense Crisis for Saskatchewan Farmers

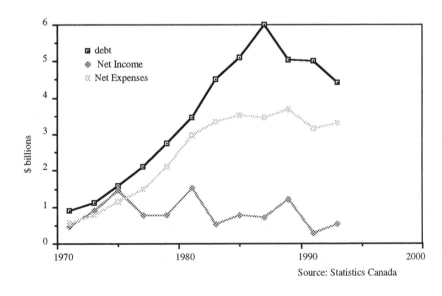

Source: Statistics Canada

38

larger social relationships. Their character was determined by other factors such as religion or custom. When markets were linked, the economic dimension was taken out of its social context and reformed into a new space called "the economy." Rather than society determining economic relationships, the economy now determined social relationships. Society was re-formed in the image of the market. This is how ethics came to be separated from economics. The market is a place of transactions. All relationships became transactions. Moral concern was just a factor bidding up the price. Under this revolutionary change and influence, community was reduced to a set of commercial transactions. Under the new imperative of the market, communities were ripped up, transplanted and destroyed on a regular basis.

This is the story of the Scottish emigration following the enclosure of the common grazing lands. Its the story of the Irish emigration following the potato famine. Its the story of the mass migration of rural people to the factory towns when welfare was cut off in the countryside. It is the reality that Charles Dickens described and Karl Marx analysed. The joining of markets can release forces more powerful than a January blizzard. When markets are linked to form a new market system, economic forces break through the corrals erected to protect the people from them. The roads are no longer safe. Local people find they are no longer in control and can no longer channel these forces to a common purpose. The communities that have grown up on the assumption that these forces can be and have been harnessed, are swept aside. It should come as no surprise that farmers are protesting the loss of community. Their feelings are justified. Their communities really are being lost.

Family is the smallest and most intimate form of community. Families that conform to our ideal are freely chosen relationships that exist for mutual love and support. They also provide a context for the development and nurture of the next generation of humanity. From the point of view of the market though, they are primarily economic units. From the market perspective they are consumer buying clubs benefiting from the cheaper prices available by buying in bulk. When individuals lose control over economic forces, they become unable to sustain their routines of family life. Just as in larger social units, the triumph of the market means the dislocation of the community of the family.

Globalization is a powerful new social reality that rearranges the power structure in our society. It has re-inforced the power and enriched the lives of some and threatened the livelihood and impoverished the lives of many others. Since it is a human creation and a social rather than a natural fact, it lies within the realm of human choice. We can support it or resist it. We can approve it or condemn it. What this means is that globalization is now a fundamental moral concern.

The Ethics of Globalization

Carl Jung once said that the root of human evil was the refusal to become conscious. Insofar as we refuse to become conscious of the origins and consequences of this new human creation called globalization, we have the potential to let evil run free. At the moment, that is the direction in which we seem to be headed. In spite of former President Bush's overheated rhetoric that the new world order is an "American" order, the reality seems to be that we are now heading out of the historical period sometimes known (ironically) as *Pax Americana*. The new world is the world of globalization. The forces unleashed by this new unregulated world have caused governments and large corporate voices to join in a unified chorus. The song is a song of competitiveness.

It is important to remember that competitiveness as an issue is not a new one. Trade and commerce have always been about competition. What is new is the idea that competitiveness is the *only* issue. When competitiveness stands alone among our concerns it becomes not an economic factor, but an over-arching ethic. It is being promoted as our over-riding guide to action. It is our norm for behaviour. One of the reasons why this argument has such a hold on us is the belief that the opposite of competitiveness is un-competitiveness. Un-competitiveness means a lower standard of living, and no one wants that. If we were talking only about economic factors, this would be a true statement, but when we elevate competitiveness to a single over-riding concern it ceases to be a factor and becomes an ethic. For this reason it is important to understand that the opposite of competitiveness is not un-competitiveness. The opposite of an ethic of competitiveness is an ethic of cooperation.

Everything is now being judged by what effect it will have on our competitive position (see Porter 1990).[8] All of these issues are translated into factors in the cost of production. Companies now demand that unions "roll back" their wages and benefits or they will move their plants to the U.S. or Mexico. These same pressures apply to farm income. Supply-management systems which support farm livelihoods are now described as obstacles to competition. For example we are being told that universal medical care is now an obstacle to our competitiveness. Progressive rates of taxation, requiring citizens to pay according to their ability, puts our country at a competitive disadvantage. Legislation which is proposed to strengthen the rights of workers is now opposed on the grounds that it will weaken our competitive position. The net effect of this isolation and elevation of competitiveness as the dominant moral norm is to subordinate questions of social justice to questions of economic efficiency. Instead of asking what is the most economically efficient means of establishing a just society, we are now asking how much social injustice are we prepared to tolerate to establish an efficient economy.

All ethics are guides for action. The ethic of competitiveness, when it stands alone atop the pyramid of our concerns, produces an activity of domination. Each agent seeks not just to win, but to win completely. We seek to put our competitors out of business. We seek to dominate the industry. This activity of domination is vertical as well as horizontal. We seek not just to dominate our neighbours, when it comes to agriculture, we also seek to dominate the land. We seek production without limits. The only way we will discover any limits to this activity is by putting the land out of business—by killing it.

The opposite of domination is solidarity. Solidarity is a form of friendship. We cannot be friends with those we seek to dominate. We cannot stand in solidarity with those we are trying to put out of business. When it comes to the land, we cannot be friends with the earth if we are seeking production without limits. An ethic of competitiveness in Olympic competition produces athletes on steroids. An ethic of competitiveness in agriculture produces a massive increase in chemical-based agriculture. What we have now is agriculture on steroids. An ethic of competitiveness in agriculture is an ethic of domination. An ethic of competitiveness makes social solidarity a liability internationally, nationally and environmentally.

In order for solidarity to be renounced, compassion must be replaced by indifference. We cannot afford to care about the losers in the race to become competitive. We are being told that our social programs are a problem because they make us less competitive. The 1980s was a decade that saw seven years of uninterrupted economic growth. It was also the decade that saw Canadians harvest a devastating new crop—food banks. This decade witnessed the simultaneous growth of wealth and poverty. We are being told that we can't afford to care. The connections between food banks and fast cars must be obscured.

Ethics of Globalization

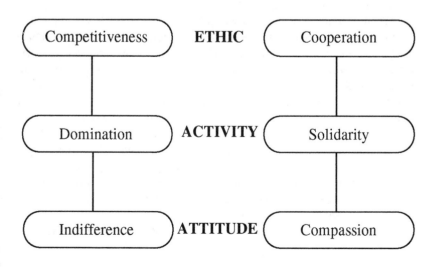

41

What is to be done?

We must replace competition with cooperation. It is possible to increase trade in an atmosphere of cooperation with the criteria of mutual benefit and reciprocity. What would cooperation with nature look like? What would mutual benefit to nature look like? One test might be agricultural practices that enhance the fertility of the soil and that share the resources with other life forms/living systems. This would be a departure from current practice to be sure but some bold initiatives are called for. Deregulating the international financial system is like camping on the prairie when it is -40°C, because it is cheaper than building a house. What is required is a rebuilding of the house.

An ethic of cooperation caused our ancestors to raise barns together in a celebration of community. A renewed ethic of cooperation would be one necessary step toward a rebuilding of these shelters and a reconstructed community.

We must replace domination with solidarity. In social policy this means seeking control over economic change in order that everyone shares in the benefits. It means judging the effects of economic change from the perspective of the least advantaged. It means forming partnerships with low income and disadvantaged groups so that their voices might be heard. In agriculture this means forming alliances with farm groups resisting the transformation from community-based agriculture to corporate agriculture. It means controlling environmental changes so that nature also benefits from them.

We must replace indifference with compassion. In social policy this means replacing food banks with an adequate social welfare system. This might mean an increased minimum wage, or increased welfare rates, or a guaranteed annual income. Overcoming indifference in agriculture would mean treating farms and farmers not as mines and miners but as partners in creation and as experts in environmental conservation.

Whether or not globalization was the product of a single intention, it is clearly a human creation. It does not arise from natural law. We are free human beings with the power to influence our destiny. We have knowledge of the difference between good and evil which means we must take responsibility for our choices. Regardless of how we evaluate it, we produced it. In that context, how we evaluate it morally becomes of crucial importance. Is it a good thing or a bad thing? Do we rejoice at its appearance or do we dread its advance? My own view is that what is of critical importance is the way we respond to it. If we surrender our self-determination on its doorstep, then it becomes an instrument of death. If it enhances our ability to create a more just society, then it becomes an instrument of life. It is already clear that it is a powerful new vortex that may drive thousands of new economic turbines—but it may also suck millions of unsuspecting victims into a dark hole.

One of those unsuspecting victims was my seatmate during the National

Farmers Union annual convention in January 1993. He was an indeterminate number of years past sixty, his grey hair swept back from his weather beaten face. In front of him his hands were folded like gnarled tree roots eroded into view. We had just been listening to a panel talk about strategies for dealing with farm debt. At the break he turned to me and said he had gone before the Farm Debt Review Board in 1988. He had walked out of there having lost title to all of his land. This was followed by a heart attack, cataracts, and arthritis. His chest began to heave with sobs. He had just discovered there were seven other options he didn't know anything about.

Saskatchewan farmers are responding to some very powerful and very deep trends. They have intuited that this crisis is not just a crisis like other crises. They have sensed their own abandonment. Without understanding the details of globalization they have challenged current trends which sever the traditional connection between agriculture and sovereignty. After years of blaming themselves and their neighbours for debt on the farm, they are beginning to understand that present farm debt was not caused by farmers but by the revolution in the international financial system. When they call for a renewal of the cooperative spirit and vision, they are challenging all of us to take responsibility and make conscious decisions about the shape of the future. [9]

Notes

1. See also the Spring 1993 issue of the journal *Theological Education* which is focussed on "Globalization and the Classical Theological Disciplines."
2. "In its simplest definition, globalization means that suppliers and demanders of capital no longer need to be in the same place to strike deals. Globalization is a process that was made possible by deregulation, including the lifting of restrictions on capital movement, but rendered necessary since the mid-1970s by the need to recycle large financial surpluses linked to large trade imbalances, involving first the OPEC countries and, lately, Japan." Theirry Noyelle, Senior Research Scholar and Assoc. Director of the Conservation of Human Resources Project, Columbia University (1989: 94-95).
3. Others also see this parallel. Alexander King and Bertrand Schneider, in their 1991 report to the Club of Rome (p. xix.), put it this way: "We are convinced that we are in the early stages of the formation of a new type of world society which will be as different from today's as was that of the world ushered in by the Industrial Revolution from the society of the long agrarian period that preceded it."
4. One example of an attempt to manage currency values is the accord reached by the finance ministers and central bank governors of the G-5 countries at the Plaza Hotel meeting, September 25, 1985. The United States, Great Britain, West Germany, France and Japan make up the G-5 nations. See Funabashi 1989.

5. Michael Lewis described the event this way: "On October 6, 1979, Volker announced that the money supply would cease to fluctuate with the business cycle; money supply would be fixed, and interest rates would float . . . in practice, the shift in the focus of monetary policy meant that interest rates would swing wildly. . . . Overnight the bond market was transformed from a backwater into a casino." See Michael Lewis (1989:35).

6. Records of bank brokerage mergers are reproduced in Hamilton 1986.

7. For an analysis of Japan's attempt to control the price of the Yen on international markets, see Funabashi 1989.

8. For more on how Karl Polanyi's analysis can be used to interpret the social impact of economic change, see Lind 1990.

9. Susan George makes the same point in her book on the environmental implications of Third World debt. "We have indeed met the enemy and he is not so much 'us' as the people and the institutions we have allowed to speak for and to represent us. Only informed and active citizens can call them to account" (1992:33).

CHAPTER TWO

Moral Economy and Market Society

The Rosetown Rally

It was a Saturday when Helen, a former student, phoned—out of the blue it seemed to me. It was a surprise since this was September and my first sabbatical had started three months earlier. This year I wouldn't have to deal with students.

"Are you still doing research on the farm crisis, Chris?"

"Sure am." I replied. "That and too many other things."

"I suppose that means you'll be at the rally on Monday."

"What rally?"

"You mean you haven't heard? The one the farmers are having down in Rosetown." My heart sank a little. I had other plans for Monday and I wasn't sure I would have access to a car that day.

"Who's organising it?"

"A bunch of guys from near where we farm."

"Do you know them?"

"Of course I know them. I went to school with most of them. It's funny, you know, half of these guys have never talked in front of a microphone before in their lives. They'd be too scared! And here they are organising a farm rally at the Rosetown rink." Helen had a good laugh. It was genuine amusement mixed with a fair measure of pride.

"Are you going to be there yourself?" I asked. I always hate to go to big, strange gatherings alone.

"Sure. Reg and I will be driving over from the farm."

Helen and Reg's farm is about half an hour from Rosetown and that meant I wouldn't be able to get a ride from her. They also have a house in Saskatoon that Helen has been living in while she was studying for the ministry.

"Would you be able to introduce me to the organisers if I went?"

"Sure. I'd be happy to. I can introduce you to all of them."

"Well, Helen, I know that I need to interview farmers for my research and I know that I need to start with that piece. But I also feel like I've been waiting for something to happen and maybe this is what I've been waiting for. I'll see you there."

It's a two hour drive from Saskatoon to Rosetown. It was a bright, sunny day. The fields were bragging their autumn brushcuts and the big, round bales meant the season's record crop had been harvested in good time. I settled in and listened to CBC Morningside talk about two-dollar wheat and the farm protests erupting across the West. Sandy McNab from Minnedosa, Manitoba was being interviewed. He had helped organise the Brandon rally. There was another rally scheduled for Winnipeg on October 9. Gzowski carries his Moose Jaw newspaper experience like a talisman around his neck. He rubs it firmly and regularly as a way of getting back in touch with the world beyond Metro. You can hear it.

I'm still not used to the way people give directions in the countryside. Everything's " . . . down about two miles and left on the grid road. You can't miss it!" Nothing fills me with a greater sense of dread than realising I'm going to be the first person in forty years to "miss it." The rally was at the rink. "You can't miss it," I was told. Well, actually you can't. Not when all the cars and trucks are headed in the same direction.

The rally was due to start at 1:00 p.m. and I had gotten a good start, arriving early enough to have lunch beforehand. I thought I'd find the rink first and then look for lunch. Good thing, too. The rink's an enormous quonset hut on blocks. The second biggest building in town after the grain elevators. Home of the Rosetown Redwings—winner of so many league championships they're running out of room for the pennants. When I arrived at 12:30 they had also run out of parking space for the cars. The presence of buses suggested that this might be bigger than I had expected.

I lined up to go in, placing a contribution in the barrel stationed at the front door for that purpose. The hallways were more like tunnels, dark and cold. They slowly expelled us in a seemingly endless stream into a corner of the rink. A playoff hockey game could probably draw four thousand people into the rows of wooden seats fastened to concrete steps surrounding the ice. But it was too early for ice and the cement floor had been divided in half and filled with chairs to create an amphitheatre effect. Clearly, the organisers were expecting about fifteen hundred people.

Most everyone there was a farmer—either a farmer or a journalist. The men wore cowboy boots, jean jackets and caps decorated with logos like John Deere, Co-op and Hoechst. The women wore trousers and warm coats. The television technicians wore jeans and beards. The journalists wore make-up.

Just before 1:00 p.m. one of the organisers announced that the start of the meeting would be delayed to allow everyone to be seated. A cheer went up from the crowd that now clearly exceeded what the organisers had expected. The river of rallyers was continuing to push into the rink. I hadn't found Helen yet and I didn't want to risk wading into the crowd and having trouble getting back. Another organiser announced another delay and was greeted by more enthusiastic applause. Eventually every seat in the arena would be filled and half the floor as well. This was special.

Members of the media were reminded to pick up copies of the speeches at the head table. I decided to assume that identity and mill about on the floor of the arena where Helen might be able to spot me. I busied myself taking photographs of the multitude including those who had already prepared their remarks on placards. One of them read, "Break the farmer—Break the nation."

I wanted to listen to what was being said with a special set of ears. I wanted to hear what people thought was morally wrong, not just technically/economically wrong. The Prime Minister was starting to heat up the constitutional pot again. This placarded farmer was making what seemed to me to be a powerful and direct appeal to the Prime Minister's agenda. With one slogan he was identifying a category of citizen that cuts across linguistic, ethnic, and regional boundaries. He was identifying the significance of the farmer's activity within the national structure as a whole. "Break the farmer—Break the nation." He was saying this was wrong.

When the rally eventually started, they began by singing "O Canada," the national anthem.

Helen and Reg found me. They had saved me a seat on the floor of the arena, five rows in front of the placard and three rows behind someone everyone was craning their necks to see. It turned out to be Roy Romanow, the leader of the New Democratic Party in Saskatchewan.

Grant Devine was Premier of Saskatchewan through most of the 1980s. He had been spinning out the final days of his second term desperately hoping an agricultural miracle would save his political bacon. The 1980s had seen a precipitous decline in rural fortunes but Grant had a Ph.D. in agricultural economics and belonged to the same Conservative party as the Prime Minister. Rural voters had been pursuaded in 1986 that he could do better than an NDP government largely unchanged from the one that had been defeated in 1982. A big federal grant to farmers had been announced just prior to the last election day. People were wondering whether history would repeat itself. The same John F. Kennedy good looks that attracted so much national attention during the constitutional conferences ten years earlier had always been a handicap for Romanow in rural Saskatchewan. This time the Tories were attempting to ridicule his urban background by attaching signs to farm machines near NDP rallies which read "Roy, this is tractor." Roy needed to be here and he was.

The other politician who ended up at the microphone was Lynda Haverstock, the neophyte leader of the Liberal party in Saskatchewan. A professional psychologist by training, Lynda had done important but little-known work documenting farm stress. She needed to communicate her commitment to farm families if the Liberals were going to return any members to the provincial legislature. She needed to be here and she was.

It was hard to miss the fact that Roy and Lynda had come. They took turns being surrounded by the electrified press—videocams, television lights, microphones and yards of black and orange cables. I was wondering whether this was going to turn into an anti-government rally of one sort or another. As it turned out the inexperienced organisers of the rally had anticipated this development. They had insisted that only the previously designated speakers would be given platform time. This was a farmers' rally and it was farmers who would do the talking. If the politicians wanted to come and listen, fine. If they wanted to speak, they'd have to take their turn at the mike like everyone else. Time limit is two minutes, no exceptions. Anybody using the time just to harangue the government, any government, would be cut off.

The organisers were mostly successful. The politicians did take their turns and a few people were cut off. Exceptions were made if the governments you wanted to harangue were American or European. At least one politician did come just to listen—the federal Minister of Agriculture, Bill McKnight. He sat to the side, listened to the presentations, avoided the press, and left early to catch his plane back to Ottawa.

The organisers had prepared presentations, short and to the point. Then the microphones were opened to all comers. The message was fairly straight forward. It's the best and worst of times. Area farms are producing their biggest harvest ever. Some are producing fifty bushels an acre where thirty-five is considered a good crop. On the other side of the ledger though, "we are forced to accept $2 per bushel for the best damn wheat in the world" (the lowest price in Canadian history).

But there are other more complex themes being woven into the fabric of this rally. The farmers are clearly asking for an end to the international trade war that's depressing the world wheat price and they're also asking the government for $30 per seeded acre as a fulfillment of Mulroney's promised "third line of defence." But they're justifying this support on a different basis. "We do not want to be thought of as welfare cases," one of the first speakers exclaims. "There isn't one farmer in this building who wouldn't rather get a fair price for wheat and forget all the subsidies," says another.

They are saying that farming is an essential activity that one part of society does on behalf of the rest and therefore, all of society is obligated to treat that group fairly. "The most important thing is growing food. Please help us out." "Farmers are supporting consumers across Canada." "We're not Saskatchewan farmers, we're Canada's farmers." They're saying that the current arrangement of economic affairs is morally wrong. "What these countries are doing to us is internationally immoral and an abomination on world trade." "Stop this debilitating madness and start trading fairly." And they are expressing their anger about it and their willingness to take action to change it. "Let's not fall into the abyss without a damn good fight."

My hunch was right. The formal market (economic) analysis was scattered and contradictory. The moral analysis was thorough and consistent. These farmers who had never stood in front of a microphone before were appealing to moral categories they assumed would be generally understood. They were pointing to the ethical cloth that formed the backdrop to the marketplace that had gone so wrong. They were trying to give voice to the moral economy that gave meaning to their lives and livelihood.

The Moral Economy

Moral economy is a term that has been re-introduced into modern scholarship by the British historian E.P. Thompson. Thompson is most well known for his book *The Making of the English Working Class* (1965). An even more relevant document is his article, "The Moral Economy of the English Crowd in the Eighteenth Century" (1961). In this, Thompson is arguing against those historians who interpret the actions of the rioting eighteenth century crowd as nothing more than a spasmodic response to hunger. Instead, he writes, "It is possible to see in almost every eighteenth century crowd action some legitimizing action." He means by this that, "The men and women in the crowd were informed by the belief that they were defending traditional rights or customs; and, in general, that they were supported by the wider consensus of the community" (Thompson 1961: 78). These traditional rights and customs had to do with what were considered legitimate and illegitimate practices when it came to marketing, milling, baking, the prices charged for these products or services, and the proper economic roles of different members of the community. All of these taken together constitute what Thompson calls "the moral economy of the poor" (79).

In the article, Thompson quotes example after example of attempts by ordinary people to re-establish customary prices for goods (like bread or corn) now in short supply. The prices established were often directly related to statutes enacted a century earlier on how corn shall be sold in times of scarcity.[1] Similarly, as regional, national, and even international markets for grain were established, there were often riots when landowners attempted to transport the grain. According to custom, prices were fixed, all grain had to be offered for sale in the local open market, and the poor were given the first opportunity to purchase the grain in small quantities at these prices, prior to the dealers who might buy all the remainder. The new practices of price-setting markets, and grain sold standing in the field or by sample, were direct assaults on the traditional rights of the poor.

In his 1991 book, *Customs in Common*, Thompson quotes the sheriff of Gloucestershire who in 1766 observed a crowd going

> to a farmhouse and civilly desired that they wou'd thresh out and bring to market their wheat and sell it for five shillings per bushel, which being promised, and some provisions given them unasked for, they departed without the least violence or offence. (227)

Thompson describes a crowd, in 1795, in Oxfordshire, stopping a wagon and setting a price of forty shillings a sack. Fifteen sacks were purchased in this manner and a local constable was entrusted with the money (229). In the same year in Essex, a baker was stopped by over forty women and children who offered him 9d (nine pence) a loaf. He demanded 19d. "They then 'swore that if he would not let them have it at 9d a Loaf, they would take it away, and before he could give any other Answer, several Persons then about him took several of the Loaves off his Pads. . .' Only at this point did Smith agree to the sale at 9d the loaf" (235).

Women regularly participated in these moral protests and were often leaders. Thompson describes a scene in Nottingham in 1812 where, "The women paraded with a loaf upon a pole, streaked with red and tied with black crepe, emblematic of 'bleeding famine decked in Sackecloth'" (257).

The moral economy of the poor, according to Thompson, was based on the paternalist model (1961: 95) and derived from the locally-based subsistence economy (98). The normal assumption was that food grown in a region should be consumed in that same region. In times of scarcity it was the duty of those in power to protect the provisioning ability of the poor. It was the export of foodstuffs during these times that especially provoked the poor to riot. The policy was elaborated during the reign of Elizabeth I and codified in the *Book of Orders* in 1630 during the reign of Charles I. The law made the magistrates the agents of enforcement with the power to order grain into the market and ensure fair prices. This practice had fallen into disuse during the Civil Wars but the policy was popular and lived on in popular memory. One hundred and fifty years later it was being appealed to and enforced by the crowd if not by the magistrate. Of course, one of the consequences of this action was that it reinforced the paternalist system of authority (that is, the power of the village squires) against the rising power of the urban merchant class. However, Thompson also points out one way in which the moral economy of the poor broke decisively with the paternalistic order. The "popular ethic sanctioned direct action by the crowd, whereas the values of order underpining the paternalist model emphatically did not" (98).

The alternative model opposing the moral economy of the poor was the political economy of the free market—the policy known as laissez-faire. In Thompson's analysis, where the poor sought legitimation in the old order, the new order sought to de-legitimate or "de-moralize" trade. "The new economy entailed a demoralizing of the theory of trade and consumption no less far-reaching than the more widely debated dissolution of restriction upon usury" (89).[2] This is the separation of ethics and economics that occured in the nineteenth century that we now take for granted. We will see later that another theorist traces this shift to the eighteenth century separation of government from commerce. In Thompson's terms, "The old pamphleteers were moralists first and economists second. In the new economic theory questions as to the moral polity of marketing do not enter, unless as preamble and perorations"(90). In other terms, the pamphleteers defended socially defined needs and demanded that the economy serve them where the apologists of laissez-faire defended the market system and demanded that society accommodate it. Thompson is careful to say that when he describes political economy as "de-moralized" he is not suggesting that Adam Smith and his colleagues were immoral or unconcerned for the common good. The political economists defended the market system on the basis of its ability to meet the common good. Thompson is not concerned to malign Smith's intentions but only to remind us that "intention is a bad measure of ideological interest and of historical consequences" (89, note 48).

Since Thompson's recovery of the term "moral economy," it has been picked up by others, especially those trying to understand the reaction of peasant societies and early industrial societies to economic transformation. In response to this usage, Thompson disclaims any proprietary interest.

> The same weaving communities that were involved in food riots (1766) were involved in industrial actions (1756); these were informed by the same values, showed the same community solidarities and sanctions (such as rough music against those who broke the norms of the trade), a similar appeal to custom and to Tudor and Stuart statute law (when this protected their own interests), and a similar insistence that, where the community's economic well-being was concerned, market forces and the profits of individuals should be subdued to custom. . . .

> Of course these workers were habituated to an economy with markets, but markets conducted within customary norms; in times of conflict they affirmed the priorities of "the Trade," or they elevated the defence of the interests of the working community above those of the profits of the few, and if the term "moral economy" helps us to identify these norms and practices, then let it be used.[3] It certainly helps us to see the strongly defensive, and, in that sense, conservative nature of this plebian culture." (1991: 338)

My own use of the term in this study certainly extends Thompson's use but in a way that is, I believe, consistent with his use. Like Thompson, I am examining moments of agricultural protest as occasions when the moral norms and practices of the community are revealed. My assumption is that these norms are operative but may not be articulated in the absence of any need to do so. It is precisely the dangers inherent in economic transformation that call them into the public realm. Like Thompson I observe that these moral notions

> exist as a tissue of customs and usages until they are threatened by monetary rationalisations and are made self-conscious *as* a "moral economy." In this sense, the moral economy is summoned into being in resistance to the economy of the "free market." (Thompson 1991: 340)

If we understand what is meant by the term moral economy, we must now turn our attention to the reality against which it is reacting and protesting. That reality is the reality of market society. The best interpreter of that reality for our purposes is Karl Polanyi.

Market Society

Karl Polanyi was a Hungarian born politician, economist and economic historian (1886-1964). His reputation as an economic historian was established with the publication of his reinterpretation of the Industrial Revolution, *The Great Transformation,* in 1944. Although he built a lasting intellectual reputation among economic anthropologists, during his lifetime he also had a significant impact upon that loose network of activists and social reformers known as the Christian left. Today his work remains as one of the most significant entry points into economic analysis for those social critics who are animated primarily by moral concern for the dispossessed and disempowered.

There are three basic themes in Polanyi's work that I want to develop. The first theme is historical and is dealt with primarily in *The Great Transformation*[4]— it is the story in English economic history of the development of market economy and the creation of a market society which resulted. The second theme is theoretical and has to do with Polanyi's distinction between formal and substantive economics. It is anticipated in his article, "Our Obsolete Market Mentality" (1947), and developed more fully in his article, "The Economy As Instituted Process" (1957).[5] The third theme is methodological and has to do with Polanyi's starting point, namely, the reality of society.

Market Economy, Market Society and Moral Economy

Polanyi begins his economic inquiry with the Industrial Revolution. He is not concerned to explain that revolution itself. Many have tried and he grants that, "No one single cause deserves to be lifted out of the chain and set apart as the cause of that sudden and unexpected event" (1944: 40). He is concerned, rather, with one particular feature of it. How is it that such unprecedented material improvement could combine with such unprecedented social havoc? "Writers of all views and parties, conservatives and liberals, capitalists and socialists invariably referred to social conditions under the Industrial Revolution as a veritable abyss of human degradation" (39). His answer to this problem is as follows:

> We submit that an avalanche of social dislocation, surpassing by far that of the enclosure period, came down upon England; that this catastrophe was the accompaniment of a vast movement of economic improvement; that an entirely new institutional mechanism was starting to act on Western society; that its dangers, which cut to the quick when they first appeared, were never really overcome; and that the history of nineteenth century civilization consisted largely of such a mechanism . . . but the new creed was utterly materialistic and believed that all human problems could be resolved given an unlimited amount of material commodities. (40)

> That new mechanism was market economy. A market economy is a self-regulating system of markets and while Polanyi acknowledges that no society could exist without an economy of some sort, he argues that prior to the nineteenth century, "no economy has ever existed that, even in principle, was controlled by markets. . . . Gain and profit made on exchange never before played an important part in human economy." (43)

Using the work of anthropologists Malinowski and Thurnwald, Polanyi argued that the assumptions that informed Adam Smith about earlier societies were quite mistaken. Smith thought that humans had a natural "propensity to barter, truck and exchange one thing for another" (43). This meant a tendency to create markets and to operate on what we now refer to as market principles.

Using this argument, a market economy would merely express in economic terms truly human nature. In response, Polanyi argued that,

> The outstanding discovery of recent historical and anthropological reserarch is that man's economy, as a rule, is submerged in his social relationships. He does not act so as to safeguard his individual interest in the possession of material goods; he acts so as to safeguard his social standing, his social claims, his social assets. He values material goods only in so far as they serve this end. (46)

In this respect, Smith's assumptions about "economic man" (sic) were "more relevant to the immediate future than [they were] to the dim past" (44) (Adam Smith's *Wealth of Nations* was published in 1716).

Smith's principles of barter, truck, and exchange depend for their effectiveness, Polanyi argued, on the existence of a market pattern. The more limited the scope of markets, the more limited the scope of these so-called "natural tendencies." Polanyi was not arguing that people will not or do not barter. Rather he was saying the societies may be organised to give prominence to any number of principles, even reciprocity or redistribution. Similarily, these principles may exist in a society without being the most prominent ones. The real historic pattern, he said, was that economic relationships were embedded in social relationships. Markets existed and, "from the sixteenth century onwards they were both numerous and important. . . . [But] the very idea of a self-regulating market was absent" (55). What was revolutionary about nineteenth century England was that economic motives were made to dominate over social relationships and so the historic pattern was inverted.

This transformation occured as isolated markets were linked to form a market system. This linkage occured as commerce and industry demanded it. As trade improved, markets for the same commodity were linked geographically. With the advent of the factory system markets for all the commodities necessary for industrial production were linked through the factory. The most important of the commodities necessary for industrial production, Polanyi argues, were labour, land and money. This is a crucial point for Polanyi because these are not commodities in the normal sense since they are not goods produced for sale. However the factory system demanded that these essential elements be available for purchase. The consequence was that labour, land and money were organised on market principles with prices being set by buyers and sellers. Since labour is just another word for humanity and land is just another word for nature, it meant that society would now be reorganised to conform with the demands of the market. Market economy had produced market society.

According to Polanyi, the last of the markets to be created was the market for labour. The Act of Settlement of 1662 had tied labour to the parish. People couldn't travel the country looking for work. This act was altered in 1795 and, with parish sefdom now abolished, might have permitted the development of a national labour market except for the introduction that same year of an "allowance system" known as the Speenhamland law. The policy worked out at Speenhamland in Berkshire established an allowance from the poor rates tied to the price of bread. This differed from previous law insofar as it provided a guaranteed minimum income for the employed as well as the unemployed and was given as outdoor relief, not committing the person to the workhouse. Previously, relief was only provided to those unable to find work.

While "no measure was ever more universally popular" (79), according to Polanyi, in the long run the result was ghastly. Although it took some time till the self-respect of the common man sank to the low point where he preferred poor relief to wages, his wages which were subsidized from the public funds were bound eventually to be bottomless, and to force him upon the rates. Little by little the people of the countryside were pauperized; the adage, "once on the rates, always on the rates" was a true saying. But for the protracted effects of the allowance system, it would be impossible to explain the human and social degradation of early capitalism." (80)

Speenhamland was in effect until the Poor Law Reform of 1834 when this "right to live" was abolished. Speenhamland reinforced the paternalistic order in the same way that the protests of the moral economy did but it also created the conditions which permitted the horror of the sudden transition to a competitive labour market. The Poor Law Reform not only rolled back relief arrangements to their 1774 pattern but did so without the essential social and moral supports that society assumed to be in place. The workhouse

was deliberately made into a place of horror . . . and staying in it was made a psychological and moral torture, while complying with the requirements of hygiene and decency—indeed, ingeniously using them as a pretence for further deprivations. . . . The very burial of a pauper was made an act by which his fellow men renounced solidarity with him even in death." (102)

Speenhamland has to be understood in relation to the development of a market economy. It was intended to benefit employees but actually benefited employers because it lowered wages. It strengthened the hold of the squires over the village poor, hindered the development of a national labour market and eventually demoralized workers. Its repeal, wrote Polanyi, was the birthday of the modern working class.

The mechanism of the market was asserting itself and clamoring for its completion; human labor had to be made a commodity. Reactionary paternalism had in vain tried to resist this necessity. Out of the horrors of Speenhamland men rushed blindly for the shelter of a utopian market economy. (102)

In the eighteenth century, one of the victories of liberalism was the separation of government from business. This was one of the preconditions for the establishment of a market economy which was finally created by linking markets into a self-regulating market system. Because this market system now included markets for the essential elements of production (not just the fruits of production, but also land, labour and money), it was able to remake society in its own image. The last precondition for the establishment of market society in the nineteenth century was the acceptance of the idea that economics should be separate from politics. Since politics is just another way of describing the social dimension of moral concern (social ethics), it was this same campaign which succeeded in separating economics from ethics.

This separation is difficult for us to trace because it is doubly complicated. The first complication is that the separation was defended as a heuristic device only, since the separation of economics from ethics was defended on moral grounds. Society had been organised along market lines in order to liberate the forces of production. Poverty was understood as a greater evil than greed and so the forces of greed were harnessed to eliminate poverty. People were not asked to pursue self-interest instead of the common good, they were asked to believe that the pursuit of self-interest would necessarily serve the common good.[6] The second complication is that the success of this argument signals the triumph of one moral theory over another. Christianity, for example, has traditionally advocated an ethic based on an evaluation of individual motives. This was especially true among Protestant groups with their emphasis on the free exercise of the individual conscience. The "formal" separation of ethics from economics demands that we transfer our concern and evaluation from motives to consequences. The dominant consequentialist moral theory is known as "utilitarianism," the assumptions of which are enshrined in the instrumentalist rationality of formal economic theory. In practice this cleavage between motives and consequences, ethics and economics, was an ideological shift representing the final dis-embedding of economic relationships from their subordinate place in society. From now on there was to be a separate sphere known as the economy. But this separate sphere was not neutral. By dis-embedding the economy from society, the relationship was inverted and social relationships came to be determined by economic ones.

Polanyi says that "chronologically, Speenhamland antedated market economy; the decade of the Poor Law Reform Act was a transition to that economy. The last period [the 1870s]—overlapping the former—was that of market economy proper" (82). By the same token these transitions are also the transitions to market society. "The congenital weakness of nineteenth century society was not that it was industrial but that it was a market society" (230).

The point of Speenhamland is two-fold. On the one hand, Polanyi is concerned to show that an economic system based on the single principle of self-interest "is entirely unnatural, in the strictly empirical sense of exceptional" (249). But showing that it is novel is not enough because apologists for the market system, today as much as in the nineteenth century, want to argue that self-interest is rational and that therefore markets are naturally occuring social phenomena which we have foolishly suppressed in the past. On these grounds, a market society would be both rational and normal.

> Whatever the desirability or undesirability of such a society on moral grounds, its practicability—this was axiomatic—was grounded in the immutable characteristics of the race. (250)

His second point is to show that we typically look at human nature and society through the prejudicial filters of nineteenth century assumptions which were themselves the product of the phenomena we are trying to understand. When we think of all human society as fundamentally determined and also economic, we are reflecting those very prejudices, since these features are themselves products of, and specific to, market society.

> Contemporary outlook tended to link the two and to assume that the determinism derived from the nature of economic motivation, according to which individuals were expected to pursue their monetary interests. In point of fact there was no connection between the two. The "determinism" so prominent in many details was simply the outcome of the mechanism of a market society with its predictable alternatives, the stringency of which was erroneously attributed to the strength of materialistic motivations." (218)

Speenhamland was an unusual period of social transition—a social anaesthetic which prevented the spread of the French Revolution, delayed the establishment of a national labour market, and re-inforced the power of paternalism (what Polanyi calls the squirearchy). It also represented the birthing time of classical economics and so the unusual features of the Speenhamland period came to influence economic thought for decades to come.

In charting the birth of a market society, Polanyi acknowledges a paradox, for in his analysis of Speenhamland and the Poor law there doesn't seem to be an appropriate economic basis for the growth of poverty in society. While the amount paid out in relief rose rapidly in the late 1700s and early 1800s, between 1818 and 1826, it fell by 25 percent. National income was rising rapidly at this time and during the 1830s total rates continued to fall steadily (98). This paradox is resolved when he finally explains,

> A social calamity is primarily a cultural not an economic phenomenon that can be measured by income figures or population statistics. ... Not economic exploitation, as often assumed, but the disintegration of the cultural environment of the victim is then the cause of the degradation. The economic process may, naturally, supply the vehicle of the

destruction, and almost invariably economic inferiority will make the weaker yield, but the immediate cause of his undoing is not for that reason economic; it lies in the lethal injury to the institutions in which his social existence is embodied. The result is loss of self-respect and standards, whether the unit is a people or a class, whether the process springs from so-called "culture conflict" or from a change in the position of a class within the confines of a society." (157)

Polanyi's point is that the social upheaval associated with the Industrial Revolution is analagous to the social upheaval of cross-cultural conflict. A society can experience cultural collapse even when the GNP increases. This corresponds to Thompson's observation that the protest of moral economy asserts the priority of the community over the individual. Individuals may prosper materially but if it occurs at the expense of the institutions of the community, social collapse may be the end result.

Market economy was born through the midwifery of economic liberalism which advocated a doctrine of laissez-faire. Since Polanyi's argument is that market economy poses a threat to the "human and natural components of the social fabric" (150), we should expect to find in the historical records spontaneous and varied attempts to protect that same social fabric. Polanyi offers just such evidence. He cites lists of all kinds of legislation (146) passed by liberals and anti-liberals, in England and elsewhere throughout Europe, at various times during the second half of the nineteenth century. He includes "factory laws, social insurance, municipal trading, health services, public utilities, tariffs, bounties and subsidies, cartels and trusts, embargoes on immigration, on capital movements, on imports, in his lists of spontaneous acts of protection" (144). His point is that market economy refashioned society but since market society is inherently unstable, our unbroken experience since that time has been of our need to re-embed economic relations within social relations.

> Our thesis is that the idea of a self-adjusting market implied a stark utopia. Such an institution could not exist for any length of time without annihilating the human and natural substance of society; it would have physically destroyed man and transformed his surroundings into a wilderness. Inevitably, society took measures to protect itself, but whatever measures it took impaired the self-regulation of the market, disorganized industrial life, and thus endangered society in yet another way. It was this dilemma which forced the development of the market system into a definite groove and finally disrupted the social organization based upon it. (3)

Moral Economy and Market Society

We can summarize Polanyi's analysis of economic history in the following way. We presently live in a society which is named after its central institution, the market, or market society. This form of social organisation is a modern invention but its ideas and justifications have profoundly shaped our own self-understanding. In particular this invention rests on three ideas. The first is that while human motives may be described as either material or ideal, it is the material motives that govern the affairs of everyday life. The second idea is that human institutions are largely determined by the economic system. The third idea is that the first two ideas are universally true—that they are true regardless of whether society has organised itself to take them into account.

Polanyi's critique begins with the third idea—that the first two ideas are timeless. Polanyi argues that in a market economy both ideas are true, but *only* in a market economy. They are true precisely because the society has been organised to promote such behavior. Because we look around and observe such behavior we are convinced that the assertions must be true. He argued that in its attempt to respond to the machine age, liberal economy (the economic thrust of liberal political philosophy) violently broke with the past by linking isolated markets of goods and creating a system of markets. Two features were novel about this market system. In the first place, the market system was thought to have its own internal logic which allowed it to operate on a self-regulating basis. This logic was the so-called law of supply and demand. The second novel feature was that this system of markets would apply not just to commodities (things produced for sale) but also to labour and land (which are either not produced, as in land, or if produced, as in labour, not for sale).

By making land or labour into commodities freely available for sale and purchase, the market and its mechanism was made to apply to them. It could now be said that there was both a supply and demand for labour and a supply and demand for land. Finally the price of these "commodities" would now be established by the interplay of these reciprocating forces.

What had happened, Polanyi argued, was that the creation of one new thing, market economy, had created a second new thing, market society. Market economy had turned society on its head. Prior to this creation, labour and land, the equivalent of humanity and nature, had been organically connected to society with the terms of their exchange set by law and customs. It was this legal and customary basis for exchange that was being reasserted by the eighteenth century English crowds of E.P. Thompson's study.

Some people have misinterpreted Polanyi on this point. Scott Cook described Polanyi as believing that, "All human behaviour prior to the nineteenth century institutionalization of the 'self-regulating' market economy ... [was] devoid of the pursuit of self-interest and [was] inherently altruistic" (Cook 1966: 328). Cook is quite wrong in this reading of Polanyi, who limits his claims thus: "In [all economic systems known to us up to the end of feudalism in Western Europe] the orderly production and distribution of goods was secured through a great variety of individual motives disciplined by general principles of behaviour. Among these motives gain was not prominent" (Polanyi 1944: 55). Economic relationships were embedded in larger social relationships and were dependent on them. The creation of market economy was the institution of productive forces, regulated by its own mechanism. This reversed the prior relationship and made society dependent on the economy. The newly created market society was a society dominated by economic motives. The application of the market mechanism to labour and land, people and nature, meant that the dominant motives for human behaviour were now to be hunger and gain. "Nineteenth century civilization chose to base itself on a motive only rarely acknowledged as valid in the history of human societies, namely gain. The self-regulating market system was uniquely derived from this principle" (30).

By linking Polanyi's work with E.P. Thompson's research we have been able to draw out the historical lessons not only for economics but also for ethics. The inversion of the relationship of economy to society is intimately related to the transformed relationship between economy and morality. Thompson's assumption is that all economies have a moral character. As we will see in the next section, Polanyi's work demands that we take an empirical approach to all relationships between humans and nature. Polanyi and Thompson taken together suggest that we move beyond the often arid debate about whether ethics and economics can relate and grapple with the empirical question, "What is the moral character of this economy and how can it be changed?"

Formal vs. Substantive Economics

In later work Polanyi pushed at the theoretical implication of his earlier historical analysis and it is out of this work that I want to develop a second theme. If our historical assumption about all societies being market societies was wrong, how then can we understand the economic process? He concluded that we needed a new tool box which treated the economy as a "social process," thereby widening the scope of our investigation. He said that humans may be capable of "economizing action" but that,

> There is no necessary relationship between economizing action and the empirical economy.... The institutional structure of the economy need not compel, as with the market system, economizing actions. The implications of such an insight for all the social sciences which must deal with the economy could hardly be more far-reaching. Nothing less than a fundamentally different starting point for the analysis of the human economy as a social process is required. (Polanyi 1957: 240)

He called what he was trying to do institutional analysis (239). His fundamentally different starting point had to do with distinguishing between the study of market phenomena (which he called formal economics) and the study of "the whole range of man's material want satisfaction" (which he called substantive economics) (241).

In an article entitled, "The Economy As Instituted Process," he defined the two meanings of the term "economic": the formal and the substantive. The formal meaning of economic

> derives from the logical character of the means-ends relationship, as apparent in such words as "economical" or "economizing." It refers to a definite situation of choice, namely, that between the different uses of means induced by an insufficiency of those means. If we call the rules governing choice of means the logic of rational action, then we may denote this variant of logic, with an improvised term as formal economics." (243)

This is what we would call today mainstream economics. The substantive meaning of economic

> derives from man's dependence for his living upon nature and his fellows. It refers to the interchange with his natural and social environment, in so far as this results in supplying him with the means of material want satisfaction." (243)

Polanyi acknowledges that his conceptual use of the substantive economy is "unfashionable" and even that all earlier attempts to achieve a naturalistic economics were unsuccessful. This was so, he argued, because no naturalistic economics can compete "with economic analysis in explaining the mechanics of livelihood under a market system" (241). His concern though, is to relativize formal economics. He sees it as a useful form of inquiry but only one of many disciplines that concern themselves with the economy. Should it become normative it may positively hinder the work of the anthropologist, the sociologist, or the economic historian. It is also on this basis that his distinction proves useful for the ethicist or moral theologian.

The formal meaning of economic implies rules governing choices made between different uses of scarce means. Formal economic analysis can prove effective within the limitations of a market system but only within that system. Formal and substantive terms will coincide, Polanyi wrote, where the empirical economy (the reference point for a substantive approach) is controlled by a system of price-making markets (the reference point for a formal approach (244).[7] Polanyi wrote,

In the whole range of economic disciplines, the point of common interest is set by the process through which material want satisfaction is provided. Locating this process and examining its operation can only be achieved by shifting the emphasis from a type of rational action to the configuration of goods and person movements which actually make up the economy. (241)

The substantive definition implies neither choice nor scarce means. From this perspective the economy "is an instituted process" (248). It is a process because it involves materials changing places or changing hands (locational movements and appropriative movements). It is instituted because it is characterized by institutions which perform specific social functions and possess specific histories. When the economic process becomes instituted, it acquires

unity and stability; it produces a structure with a definite function in society; it shifts the place of the process in society, thus adding significance to its history; *it centres interest on values, motives and policy* [my emphasis]. Unity and stability, structure and function, history and policy spell out operationally the content of our assertion that the human economy is an instituted process. (250)

Because the human economy is an instituted process, it is a process which is embedded in *both economic and noneconomic institutions*. "The inclusion of the noneconomic is vital. For religion or government may be as important for the structure and functioning of the economy as monetary institutions or the availability of tools and machines themselves that lighten the toil of labour" (250). This is what Polanyi means when he says that the market economy is historically exceptional because it has institutionalized the motive of "gain" as the principal reason for material interaction. People have acted in history in a material fashion, for religious and other reasons. In a market society it is increasingly thought to be "irrational" to act materially for reasons other than personal profit.

In summary, the formal view grew out of the specific social conditions of the eighteenth century, where the formal analysis did approximately correspond to the empirical reality. It continues to define mainstream North American economics today. Since the middle of the nineteenth century, however, society has attempted to re-embed the economic process in order to ensure its own continued existence. This is what I understand the farmers at the Rosetown rally to be doing— attempting to re-embed the economic aspect of food production within the cultural process known as agriculture and rural life. We continue to be hampered though, by the intellectual baggage of that period, namely, Adam Smith's view of innate humanity as trucking, bartering and exchanging. According to this view, if farmers can't "make a go of it," they should do something else. Polanyi has attempted to supercede the market as our frame of reference. By using a substantive approach, he has attempted to develop "a wider frame of reference to which the market itself is referable" (270).

From an ethical point of view, Polanyi's identification and development of a substantive approach to economic relationships makes a difference in at least three ways. In the first case, since formal economics enshrines the assumptions of the utilitarian ethic on which it is justified, it means that all other social values have been subordinated to the value of efficiency as it is defined by the market system (that is, the economising of self-interested behaviour). The substantive approach renews the possibility and the hope of different social and economic arrangements according to different moral values and visions. Clearly, the appeal of moral economy is an appeal to values other than the efficient deployment of capital.

Second, the substantive approach provides some of the tools for the new toolbox that will be needed if we are actually going to carry out the identification and transformation of specific moral economies as suggested in the last section. It should be noted in this regard that the term "substantive" has tended not to be used by other economists—even those directly influenced by Polanyi. I am thinking here of David Ross and Peter Usher (1986) who have contrasted the formal with the informal economy and also of Abraham Rotstein (1984) who has done the same.

The third way the substantive/formal distinction is helpful has to do with the status of discourse about ethics among practicing economists. Polanyi's description of the substantive approach as concerning itself with the "interplay of humanity with the social and natural environment" could as well be a description of the heart of social ethics. By contrast, formal economics suppresses ethical disagreement by treating as extraneous the utilitarian ethical assumptions on which the formal approach is based. This leaves neither the social space nor the conceptual or linguistic tools to engage real moral difference.

Of course, this doesn't mean that economists haven't tried to include a moral component. One of the most detailed attempts was by the Nobel prize winner, Gunnar Myrdal.[8] The distinguished Cambridge economist Joan Robinson assumed the integration of ethics and economics but, like many others, never showed exactly how this was to be done.[9] When economists criticize each other for how they handle moral commitments and evaluations, the results are sometimes sheer confusion.[10] Only under cover of the term "political economy" can economists locate the space for moral difference but even then they lack sophisticated tools for the discourse[11] since all they've managed to do is add the language of ideological struggle.[12]

Social Criticism and the Reality of Society

A third theme also follows from Polanyi's historical analysis and I have described it as methodological. Polanyi argues that the market system destroyed society as it was then known. In the process of its destruction, society was discovered. That is, society came to be seen as something that was not just achieved (bringing civilization out of chaos, for instance) but as something that could be created one way or another. Society was discovered to be something malleable, a human construct. In the case of economics, the formal market economy remade society in its own image, hence, market society.

Polanyi relativized formal economics and cautioned against it becoming normative lest it hinder the legitimate work of the anthropologist, the sociologist or the economic historian (Polanyi 1944: 241). I would also add: the work of the social critic. Polanyi was able to relativize formal economics by engaging in the methodological shift of starting with the reality of society instead of the reality of the formal economy. This methodological shift is an important one for the social critic. Polanyi showed that the market economy was historically exceptional in the sense of being unique. One of the aspects that made it exceptional was its raising up of the motive of "gain" as the principal reason for material interaction. In a market society it is increasingly thought to be "irrational" to act materially for reasons other than personal advantage. "The inclusion of the non-economic is vital," writes Polanyi, "for religion or government may be as important for the structure and functioning of the economy as monetary institutions or the availability of tools and machines themselves that lighten the toil of labour" (250).

So first of all, we can see that so-called non-economic factors and alternative motives may be crucial in the operation of any empirical economy. Second, the methodological starting point of society, rather than market economy allows for the inclusion of factors and data not normally part of the economists' trade. When the Canadian Catholic Bishops intervened in a national economic debate in January 1983, their starting point was their pastoral experience and moral concern. In this study I have begun not with the data of the market but with the moral concern of farmers involved in farm protest. It is precisely this attention to powerlessness, families in crisis and the loss of community that can become a legitimate and significant starting point when we choose to begin with society rather than with the market.

There is a third implication of the reality of society on which I also want to comment. In a paper presented in 1986, Abraham Rotstein elaborated this theme in a philosophical direction. He described Polanyi's "reality of society" as an elliptical, subtle, and complex metaphysical doctrine. He suggests that it would be a misunderstanding" ... to think of it simply in an institutional or sociological context" (Rotstein 1986: 17). Rather, for Polanyi there are three "revelations that are formative in shaping Western consciousness: knowledge of death, knowledge of freedom, and knowledge of society" (Rotstein 1986: 15). Rotstein understands Polanyi to have revised his earlier understanding of the reality of community as the relationship of persons. From Rotstein's point of view the reality of society means that the moral freedom of the individual has been fundamentally compromised in a way that we cannot avoid but we may be able to transcend.

Rotstein writes, "Power and economic value together are the moral Achilles heel, so to speak, of the complex society. They point to an alien and external realm of social existence which has been spawned by the unavoidable wishes and choices of the members of the community. We cannot turn our faces away from the moral consequences of these spheres of activity since these networks are our collective progeny. As they run loose, they may fatefully compromise others. Yet we cannot disown them for we are the constituents of that complex society" (14).

While I am not entirely in agreement with Rotstein,[13] I think there is a knowledge of the reality of society which needs to be taken into account and which is being taken into account at the level of religious ethical discourse. From my own field I can give two examples. One of the responses to the feminist critique of ethics is to develop an understanding of the moral life in terms of relationships in community rather than in terms of the accountability of power (i.e., caring rather than justice). The American feminist theologian, Carter Heyward (1982 and 1984), is an example of one person developing an ethic of mutuality though without any explicit debt to John Macmurray. Carol Gilligan's (1982) critique of the moral development theory of Lawrence Kohlberg is a secular example of this development.

A second example involves the emergence of "solidarity" as an appropriate understanding of Christian mission. This is not just a solidarity of worker with worker based on self-interest but a solidarity with the poor by the non-poor and other popular sector groups for the sake of peace and justice, otherwise known as the common good. This is a significant shift away from the older understanding of Christian mission as the conversion of the individual to a new pattern of belief. Though not articulated as such, the move within Christian circles away from individual categories based on assumptions of freedom and power toward relational, communal and social categories does reflect, I think, the knowledge of the reality of society. This knowledge is experienced as a limitation on the viability of categories of being and doing isolated from the being and doing of others. It reflects the third lesson to be drawn from Polanyi's methodological category of the reality of society as starting point and the essence of what Rotstein describes as Polanyi's metaphysical doctrine.

That third lesson is the reality of society as limitation and opportunity. It is no longer possible to think of the individual as the primary moral category whose characteristics are normative for society. Modern industrial society is now so complex and interdependent that if one had to take individual responsibility for all the moral considerations involved in every economic transaction, no one would get out of bed in the morning. Rotstein is right to suggest that there is no longer an inviolate moral space to which the individual can retreat.

The other side of the ledger is that if we can reclaim the relational side of our being, as persons-in-community, we can secure the freedom from social calamity that is a precondition for a freedom for individual expression available to all. I have already pointed to signs of this transformation in feminist moral criticism and the contemporary Christian left. The next level of engagement will be in struggles to institutionalize the solidarity we require for true mutuality.

Back to the Rally

This may seem like a long digression from the rink in Rosetown but it serves as an indication of the ideological distance that must be travelled for these farm voices to be heard. This explanation of moral economy and market society is like an intellectual amplifier. It is being used in this book to increase the volume of these rural voices so we can hear it over the regular hum of traffic outside our windows.

The rally didn't get started until almost 1:30 p.m. By 3:30 people were starting to get restless. The presentations had all been made. Bill McKnight had left. Roy and Lynda had stood in line and taken their two minutes of airtime. Roy promised to "put farming on the top of the constitutional agenda," nicely linking his concern for farmers with his reputation as a constitutional deal maker. Lynda included her professional work on farm stress as part of the solution. "You trust and believe in one another once again. I'm so pleased." The television crews had packed up, hurrying to make the six o'clock news. Kelly Crowe, a homegrown Saskatchewan journalist who made it to the national CBC, would make "The National" once again. The farmers wanted to go home. It would be a long drive.

Just as she said she would, Helen introduced me to her old high school chums, the organisers and the people at the head table. I took down names and phone numbers. Some were friendly. Some were cautious. Some didn't want to draw attention to their personal stories.

"My situation isn't nearly as bad as some people out there!" one farmer said, somewhat defensively.

"This isn't a competition for despair," I replied. Laughter. It was a start.

I gave my thanks and good-byes to Helen and Reg and allowed the crowd to manoever me out of doors. I suddenly remembered I hadn't had any lunch. There was a gas station nearby with a convenience store that promised "greaseless fried chicken." They lied but I ate it anyway.

On the drive home I wondered about the moral categories I would discover through my interviews. I wondered about singing the national anthem and the farmer and his handmade placard, "Break the farmer—Break the nation." What was the connection between nationhood and agriculture? It was a question to which I would return.

Notes

1. These emergency measures were codified in *The Book of Orders* 1630. See Thompson 1961: 108.
2. See Tawney 1938 for a thorough discussion of the moral sanctions against usury.
3. See Randall 1988 and Charlesworth and Randall 1987.
4. Polanyi's *The Great Transformation* is a complicated book, partly because he is trying to accomplish too many things in one volume. Conceivably *The Great Transformation* could be broken down into four separate topics: 1) the collapse of the international economic system; 2) the emergence of a market system and the justification of a utopian market society through political economy; 3) the rapid expansion of the market system and the counter movement to protect society and social relationships from the consequences of that expansion; and 4) the nature of fascism as a response to the collapse of the international economy produced by the contradictions inherent in the utopian vision of market society. For our purposes topics 1 and 4 will be set aside since our first theme is contained within the second and third topics and our second theme is dealt with elsewhere.
5. Posthumously published work includes Polanyi 1965, Dalton 1968, and Pearson 1977.
6. This argument has recently and succinctly been restated in Griffiths 1984.
7. From the point of view of moral discourse however, even in societies where the two coincide, there will still be a difference since formal economics will dismiss moral claims as irrelevant *a priori*, and the substantive approach will not.
8. "... by insisting on the necessity of value premises in all research, the social sciences should be opened more effectively to moral criticism. It would then be impossible to classify economics as a 'dismal science' in the sense of its being closed to moral considerations. Economists working in the conventional mode, attempting to conceal valuations basic to their research can, however, often be rightly censured in this way, and on logical grounds" (Myrdal 1969: 73).
9. "In all this kind of analysis, the notion of ethical judgement purports to be excluded and the whole exercise is put forward as a piece of pure logic. The very idea of moral implications is abhorrent to practitioners in this field.

   "All the same, even economists are human beings, and cannot divest themselves of human habits of thought. Their system is saturated with moral feeling. Those within it, who have grown used to breathing its balmy air, have lost the power to smell it. To those approaching from outside who complain that the scent is sickly, the insiders indignantly reply: 'The smell is in your own noses. Our aim is completely odourless, scientific, logical and free from value judgements'" (Robinson 1963:57).

10. For an example see Robert L. Heilbroner's claim that economics can be value free but only at the expense of any usable theory (1973), and Mark Blaug's criticism of Heilbroner (1980). Blaug actually misreads and distorts Heilbroner's argument in significant ways.

11. For one example of this, see my discussion of moral categories in the work of Andre Gunder Frank (Lind 1983).

12. It is controversial to assert that formal economic methodology suppresses ethical disagreement. Its defenders would argue that the positive/normative distinction separates ethical (normative) concern from scientific (positive) analysis. The argument is not seamless, however. Even such an articulate exponent of the postion as T.W. Hutchinson has acknowledged that the suppression of value-judgements has happened, and when it happens, it is extremely dangerous.

> It could be argued that though this authoritatively proposed rule regarding the separation of value-judgements about the objectives of policies, from 'positive' theorizing, obtained a considerable measure of observance, it brought with it the disadvantage (as, for example with Prohibition laws) that value-judgements were not always removed or distinguished, but were driven underground or remained disguised, which could be much more dangerous and confusing than their uninhibited expression. (Hutchinson 1964: 38)

I am in agreement with Hutchinson that driving the value-judgements of economic discourse underground is more "dangerous and confusing than their uninhibited expression." It is because of this that I seek their uninhibited expression.

13. I would like to respond as a member of the contemporary Christian left. First of all, I think Rotstein uncritically affirms Polanyi's tendency toward hyperbole by suggesting the knowledge of society fits within a Hegelian framework of the transformation of human consciousness analogous to the knowledge of death and freedom. Secondly, Rotstein errs in using the term "individual in community" and "person in community" interchangeably. The philosophical voice of the English-speaking protestant Christian left in the 1930s and 1940s was John Macmurray whose language of "person in community" Polanyi adopted. Macmurray would have used the terms "persons in relation" as well as "persons in community" but not "individual in community." It was precisely Macmurray's notion of personhood as a relational category not reducible to the individual in isolation that forms part of the core of his work.

CHAPTER THREE

Powerlessness, Community and the Environment: When the System Farms the Farmers

I may not know as much about the world market as some of those professionals out there, but what I do know is that it's wrong. It's all wrong and we've got to change it.

I've seen farmers who've died. They did all the spraying. I've never had a doctor tell me but the women of the community knew how he died— chemicals, kidney failure and all that.

I was glad to have the sun behind me as I headed west along the highway one more time. It had snowed just last week, Easter Sunday morning, but already some farmers had started their spring seeding. The countryside looked different and for a while I wondered if I was on the right road. Then I realized that I had never driven this road when the fields weren't painted white. All the landmarks were different now.

An hour after leaving home I passed the town that proclaims itself "biggar" than New York. Twenty minutes later I saw the row of white grain bins on the horizon.

"Take highway 51," Bill said, "and turn right after the railroad tracks. Go about seventeen and where it turns left to Hershel keep going straight."

"Oh, I remember that corner," I replied. "There's a sign there for Mozart."

There was a pause on the phone. "Right corner," he chuckled, "wrong musician. The sign's for Handel."

Saskatchewan!

I turned into the farm road and parked behind the two story stained clapboard house. As I walked toward the machinery shed a young woman turned off her tractor in the garden and queried my confident approach. Having said I was looking for Bill, she directed me to the figure bent over what looked like a fifteen-foot rack of steel combs, and returned to her work.

Bill's what you call a big man. Over six feet tall and three feet wide, his unruly gray hair and blunt demeanor give him the air of a grumpy wizard. His t-shirt was ripped and his hands were black from mechanical labour. He presented a hand in greeting. Hoping that my pause wasn't noticeable I shook it firmly.

After telling me we were driving over to his house for the interview and introducing me to his son, I realized that the woman who had acted so territorily upon my arrival was actually the proprietor of this farm. I climbed in beside the cat food in the half ton and we set off down the road.

Bill and Louise (not their real names), with their son and daughter-in-law, farm almost two thousand acres. It was hard to tell exactly since the land is divided into seven different pieces. Since their son joined the operation in 1985, they've been organic farmers. "He said he wouldn't touch those chemicals, so that was that."

The dominant culture would have us believe that ethics and economics do not, should not and cannot mix. As a result, many people believe that farm bankruptcy can only be "blamed" on the individual farmer for their failure to "compete." People who come together to protest the farm crisis are obviously rejecting this dominant view and following a different set of moral assumptions. Moments of social protest can be seen as indicating the moral dimension of economic changes otherwise obscured by the dominant, secular culture. This shift in analytical framework liberates a moral and theological critique of market society while avoiding a naive condemnation of the economic dimension of modern life, often found in the Church.

In the course of my interviews, a number of themes have emerged. Included among these themes are concerns about "powerlessness" and a related perception that the farm "community" is no longer in charge of its own destiny—that it is the farmers who are now being farmed. Later on in the interviews, after some trust has been established, concerns are also expressed about the effect of current agricultural practice on the "environment." It is these last three concerns that this chapter will address.

Powerlessness

It is clear that there is a farm crisis in Saskatchewan; what is unclear is whether the problems are solvable. If they are, are they solvable by the people and institutions that inhabit the province? The farmers involved in farm protest are clearly frustrated by their own seeming inability to affect their fortunes. For some years in the 1980s, many people took the approach that the hard times were part of a cyclical winnowing process that goes on in all industries. Some younger farmers were losing their land for sure, but many people took this as an indication of poor management ability or poor timing. The late 1980s saw several years of drought and an infestation of grasshoppers. Many experienced farmers said that all they needed were one or two good years and things would be alright again. In terms of production, the 1990 and 1991 crop years saw the second and third largest yields on record in Saskatchewan. It was after these two "good years" that many people realized that they were worse off than before. When the cost of production ranges from $5 to $7 per bushel, the farmers respond, "We are forced to accept $2 per bushel for the best damn wheat in the world."

While farmers are divided on what exactly is the "real cause," there is widespread agreement that the trade war between Europe and the United States is an important factor. The moral analysis of the farmers is that, "what these countries are doing to us is internationally immoral and an abomination on world trade." From their point of view, current practice is contrary to elementary notions of fair trade. "Stop this debilitating madness," they shout, "and start trading fairly." The widespread sense of powerlessness is internalized in the farm community. They want and expect to be able to solve their own problems but are unable to. This is expressed when they say, "We feel the blame that others seem to be putting on us."

The powerlessness of the farm community is brought home painfully when individual farmers face foreclosure brought on by banks and other financial institutions. In these cases, farmers feel abandoned by the institutions that encouraged the debt in the first place. "What protection does the farmer have? What protection does the bank have?" In many rural municipalities more than 30 percent of the farmers have appeared before either federal or provincial farm debt review agencies. Nothing evokes the theme of powerlessness better than the image of slavery and slave labour. These metaphors come easily to hand for people who work harder and harder and see fewer and fewer results. "Farm labour is slave labour." "Fifty percent of the farm population is farmer wives. Our labour is slave labour." "We can no longer work like slaves and work more and more for less and less."

Farming the Farmers

It is this widespread feeling of powerlessness that causes members of the farm community to think of themselves as objects of agricultural practice rather than as subjects. "The governments and societies of North America decided years ago that food is a given and the farming population is taken for granted. Whatever it takes to keep them producing out there . . . do it." "Food is the last thing that anybody thinks about. . . . It's like the sun coming up every day." "The farmer and his wife are now expected to work off the farm to support the farming habit." "The system is farming the farmers."

Concern for the Environment

One of the themes that emerged frequently in my interviews was a concern for the prairie soils and the prairie environment. Interestingly, this theme only emerged late in each of the conversations. In each case the farmer expressed some concern for the general state of agricultural practice with regard to the environment, then indicated the ways they had personally responded. ("I planted two and a half miles of trees this year.") This pattern held true whether I was talking to an organic farmer or one who regularly used chemical fertilizers, herbicides, and pesticides.

The most optimistic farmer thought that by comparison to other countries, Canadian farmers "provide good food at a low cost in an ecological manner." Another was more cautious indicating that "environmental consciousness is peaking . . . [and] some mistrust isn't deserved." There was considerable disagreement over which aspect of environmental degradation was a greater concern. One farmer talked of how one chemical sterilizes the soil and how some weeds have become resistant to it. Another concluded, "There are more problems with nitrates (fertilizers) than other chemicals." Still another observed that the practice of "summerfallow is the greatest threat to the environment," even though the alternative practice of continuous cropping is often associated with increased chemical use.

Most farmers thought that the farmers themselves had the greatest interest at stake in environmentally sound farming practices ("Who has a greater concern for health than me? I'm the one who has to handle the stuff." "Most of us are greenpeacers at heart."), though at least one thought that government support programs should be tied to maintaining a minimum level of fertility in the soil. The concern over declining fertility is a response to actual practice. As one farmer put it, "I try to be conservative in a lot of ways. Not only for economic reasons, but to preserve this land. It has only been farmed for eighty-five years, maybe eighty years, and I'm sure that it has deteriorated and lost half of its original nutrients. I am trying not to make it any worse than that." Others indicate that the farmers alone can't do it. The most frequently heard explanation was that economic conditions were working against good practice. One farmers said, "Farmers need to be able to afford conservation." Another suggested, "You won't get any movement to proper land husbandry until you get something that will give you some decent return." Still another described it in terms of his own story. "When we broke this land up a hundred years ago, there was 450 pounds of available nitrogen to feed plants. Do you know what's left now? I've got land with 10 pounds. I've got good land that's still around 50 or 60 pounds of available nitrogen left. We have sold 400 pounds of nitrogen in that wonderful resource called prairie land. We've sold it over the last hundred years for nothing. Now what happens? Now you've got to put that nitrogen back in and $2 wheat won't buy any nitrogen. Somebody's going to have to pay for this or it won't grow. . . . [We're] mining the land."

Environmentally-sound farming practice was not only linked to stable economics, it was also linked to stable communities. In the context of a conversation on environmental issues, one farmer indicated, "We need to be able to maintain rural communities at a minimum acceptable level." Another suggested, "There's no better incentive for good husbandry than knowing your grandchildren will inherit the land."

The farmers involved in farm protest are describing a moral economy of powerlessness where they feel blamed for problems they want to solve but cannot. Among the problems that need solving is the continuing degradation of the environment. Yet they are being denied the economic and social stability that seem to be required to affect change. Is it possible to interpret these concerns in a more systematic way and in a way that reveals positive, possible alternatives?

The Farm Crisis is an Environmental Crisis

Among the many crises contributing to the destruction of rural Saskatchewan is the crisis in the prairie environment. This crisis has several distinguishing features. These include: soil erosion by the action of wind and water, loss of soil fertility, soil salinization, soil acidification, loss of genetic diversity, and destruction of wildlife.

In 1984, the Canadian Senate, through its Standing Committee on Agriculture, Fisheries and Forestry, produced a report on the declining quality of Canadian soils. In that report, the Committee concluded, "Canada risks permanently losing a large portion of its agricultural capacity if a major commitment to conserving the soil is not made immediately by all levels of government and by all Canadians" (Sparrow 1984: 11). Though this report is referred to from time to time, no significant action has been taken to change the situation.

In 1992, the United Nations published a report which indicated that in North America, 95.5 million hectares of soil have been degraded by human activity since the end of World War II. Soil degradation is defined as "human-induced phenomena which lower the current and/or future capacity of the soil to support human life." The degree of degradation can vary from light to extreme. Light degradation can be reversed by on-farm practices such as crop rotation and minimum tillage. Moderate degradation requires more resources than the average farm can provide—such as a national program with financial incentives and technical help. Severely eroded land requires restoration beyond the ability of most developing nations. Extreme degradation means restoration is impossible. 10.6 percent of all vegetated land in North America has been degraded to varying degrees since 1945 (World Resources Institute 1992: 112–113).

Soil degradation has many causes. One of the causes is wind erosion. Saskatchewan is known for a number of natural characteristics. One of them is its big blue sky, another is its persistent, strong wind. When soil is left uncovered, that is, unplanted or otherwise exposed to the elements, the prairie wind picks up the nutrient-rich topsoil and deposits it in gullies or streams—places where it will no longer be used to nurture crops. Our conventional methods of grain farming make the land extremely vulnerable to wind erosion.

When the land was ploughed for the first time at the turn of the century, new agricultural practices were introduced to manage the dry prairie soils. One of those practices was summerfallowing. This practice involves ploughing a field and not sowing a new crop, letting it "lie fallow" for a year. In some areas fields are left fallow every other year. Some farmers use this practice to control weeds, some do it to preserve moisture. The largest benefit comes from the build up of nutrients in the short-term, especially nitrogen. "The total land now subject to summerfallow each year makes up 13%, 24% and 38% of the cultivated land in Manitoba, Alberta and Saskatchewan, respectively." (Sparrow 1984: 45) In some regions of both Saskatchewan and Alberta it tops 40 percent (110). The practice of summerfallowing in the long term results in a reduction in fertility due to the loss of top soil. Though it is difficult to accurately measure the extent of soil erosion, "it is estimated that the annual soil loss on the Prairies by wind is about . . .160 million tonnes" (111). The resulting loss of organic matter, which helps to bind the soil and retain the nutrients, means the soil blows away even more easily. It is also more vulnerable to erosion by water. "It has been estimated that some 30% of cropland (117 million tonnes) in the Prairie provinces is exposed to potentially serious productivity losses from water erosion" (108). The loss of soil fertility is not sudden but gradual and "while prairie soils are naturally high in organic matter content, they have lost nearly 45% of their original content since cultivation began there at the turn of the century" (113).

The 1984 Senate report noted, "While the native soils in parts of the prairies originally released up to 125 pounds of nitrogen per acre (140 kilograms per hectare) per year, the same soil today may deliver as low as 9 pounds per acre (10 kilograms per hectare) if nitrogen fertilizer has not been used" (46). But wind erosion is not the only factor leading to fertility loss. The tilling of fields in preparation for leaving it fallow has resulted in the release of much more nitrogen than is used by the next crop. A recent report prepared for the Royal Society of Canada suggests that two-thirds of the nitrogen released in this way and at least some of the phosphorous, are not used by the crops (Stewart and Tiessen 1990: 194).

The amount of fertilizer used in Canadian agriculture is significant and increasing. From 1979 to 1989 Canadian farmers increased their fertilizer use from thirty-eight kilos per hectare to forty-seven kilos per hectare, an increase of 24 percent (World Resources Institute 1992: 274). In Saskatchewan, between 1971 and 1989, the amount of fertilizer used increased by over six times (see Figure 2.1). This increase in the use of imported fertility, particularly nitrogen fertilizer, masks the degradation of natural fertility because agricultural production has increased. For example, between 1980 and 1990, cereal production in Canada increased by 19 percent (272). But the increased fertilizer use contributes to environmental degradation because it decreases naturally occuring fertility and increases soil acidification. As the entymologist Stuart Hill put it, "The application of highly soluble nitrogen fertilizers to soil inhibits free living and symbiotic nitrogen-fixing organisms. The growth of the vegetation then becomes dependent on these artificial inputs" (Hill 1991: 213). In other words, the nitrogen fertilizer depresses the activity of existing organisms essential for the production of naturally occuring nitrogen. The excess application of nitrogen fertilizer also leads to ground water contamination (Dearborn 1991: 37).

The increasing acidity of soils can be caused by the chemical reactions that result from the heavy use of nitrogen fertilizers, as well as by the application of sulphur and by acid rain. It is counteracted by the application of lime. Though it is a greater problem in Eastern Canada, in Western Canada it is estimated that "a minimum of . . . 350,000 tonnes of lime per year are needed just to maintain the present pH levels of the most affected soils" (Sparrow 1984: 117).

Increasing salinity of the soil is considered by some to be the major soil degradation problem in the Prairie provinces. Here too, the practice of summerfallow is implicated. Summerfallow reduces the organic content of the soil which makes the soil less able to retain moisture. This causes the water table to rise, especially on low lying land, bringing the salts to the surface. Salinization "is a problem which usually occurs in small areas of 2 to 25 acres . . . but when all of these small occurrences are added together, they total some 5.4 million acres . . . in Canada's dryland regions. . . . Although there are differences of opinion among soil scientists, it appears that Canada's . . . salinized soils are being extended at a rate of some 10% yearly" (114).

If the increased use of fertilizer on Canadian farms is dramatic, the increased use of herbicides and pesticides is more so. In the seven years between 1977 and 1984, pesticide and herbicide use in Canada as a whole doubled from 26,928 tonnes to 54,767 tonnes. As Figure 2.1 shows, pesticide and herbicide use in Saskatchewan increased by almost ten times between 1971 and 1989.[1] Though chemical use declined somewhat with the worsening financial crisis, with the slow improvement in crop prices since 1991, chemical use has also rebounded.

The Senate Report on Agriculture called for a concerted effort to combat soil erosion by all levels of government. But more than that was required, they said, "The changes which must occur in prairie agricultural practices are nothing short of an 'agricultural revolution'" (Sparrow 1984: 51).

Increased chemical use (fertilizer, herbicides, and pesticides) is not only a mask hiding the alarming drop in soil fertility, it is also a symbol of the industrial approach to agriculture. In seeking to solve problems in the international agricultural market, some people want to strengthen the industrial approach. If the market yields low prices, this logic encourages more chemical inputs in order to boost production. It is critical though, to understand that the market system as

Figure 3.1
Chemical Use on Saskatchewan Farms

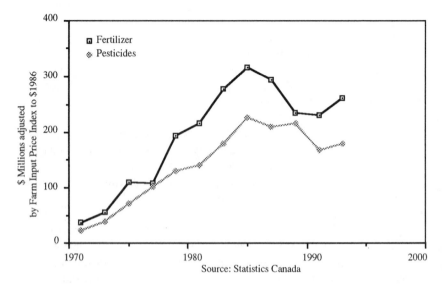

Source: Statistics Canada

a whole emerged as a response to the problems generated by industry. Consequently, an industrial approach and a market approach are essentially the same thing.

Although the Senate Report gently suggests that the problem may be policies that are having unintended effects, they also conclude, "One of the major drawbacks to soil conservation has been the emphasis on increased production. This has resulted in the creation of policies which have ignored or unintentionally worked against good soil management."[2]

When viewed against the backdrop of the history of agricultural policy, the suggestion of effects being unintended is not believable. In 1967, the federal Minister of Agriculture commissioned a Task Force to recommend policy for Canadian agriculture in the 1970s. This Task Force identified technological development as "the primary world wide force causing change. . . . This trend promised not only to continue indefinitely, but also to accelerate" (Federal Task Force on Agriculture 1969: 1). The Task Force identified not only what might happen in Canadian agriculture but also what should happen. Their model for 1990 included "decreasing . . . farm population; fewer family farms; increasing farm size;. . . [and] constant improvement in quality of management."

In what must strike today's farmers as an ironic note, the Report also predicted "rising incomes . . . [and] fewer government subsidies and support programs" (8). This is in spite of the fact that they also acknowledged, "Growing specialization and investment will make farmers increasingly vulnerable to crop, price and financial hazards" (250).[3]

These changes were designed to achieve the same kind of efficiencies in agriculture that had been achieved in manufacturing because they were both understood to be just different forms of industry. The Task Force predicted that "By 1980 agriculture—both farming and agribusiness—will be a much more trim, stable, efficient and self-reliant industry than it is at present" (263). The crowning symbol of the transformation was their recommendation that the department of agriculture be renamed the department of agricultural industry. "All of its planning and operations for commercial agriculture must be integrated around a central concept of a profit-oriented, self-sustaining industry serving the needs of all its major stakeholders adequately and fairly" (444).

Current government policy has still not come to terms with the contradictions inherent in an industrial approach to agriculture. The United Nations Report identifies industrial agriculture as one of the major threats to the worldwide loss of biological diversity (World Resources Institute 1992: 130). The doctrine of comparative advantage, first articulated by David Ricardo in the nineteenth century and recently recapitulated by Harvard economist Michael Porter for the Canadian government, requires individual farmers and nations alike to specialize in a few crops so that they can maximize production for an export market. This is the mechanism by which the number of crop species declines along with supporting species and local knowledge (135).[4] Yet the U.N. Report also endorses the principle features of market economy which are central to industrial agriculture. It criticizes attempts to manage farm prices because they "distort" prices—that is, they distort price setting markets. At the same time they recommend taxes, fees and incentives because they change behaviour. Sustainability is not a matter of morality but self-interest, and so the problem is identified as farmers who "have not been forced to take adequate account of the real costs of environmental degradation" (108). The industrial approach and the market approach go hand in hand. In order to effectively respond to the farm crisis we need to simultaneously shelter ourselves from the storm of market forces while we seek an alternative to an industrial approach.

An Ethic of Land as Community

One person who has tried to find an alternative to the industrial approach to agriculture is Aldo Leopold. Leopold (1887—1948) was an American naturalist, forester and conservationist who is looked to by some as the founder of the modern ecology movement. He is most well known for a book of essays that was published one year after his death. *A Sand County Almanac* included what became his most well known essay, "The Land Ethic." This essay was originally conceived in 1924. Leopold had just moved to Madison, Wisconsin, to become Associate Director of the Forest Products Laboratory. As he put it, "I found the industrial *motif* of this otherwise admirable institution so little to my liking that I was moved to set down my naturalistic philosophy . . ."(quoted in Callicott 1987: 285).

The key to Leopold's land ethic is his concept of community and humanity's place in it. Working on the premise that all ethics restrain freedom of action because an individual belongs to a community of interdependent parts, Leopold proposed enlarging "the boundaries of the community to include soils, water, plants, animals, or collectively, the land" (Leopold 1966: 219). The implication of this deceptively simple shift is that humans must change their role from conqueror of the community to citizen.

Industry required a market system and the market system required all social relationships to be governed by economic self-interest. From Leopold's point of view, "A system of conservation based solely on economic self-interest is hopelessly lopsided. It tends to ignore and thus eventually to eliminate, many elements in the land community that lack commercial value, but that are (as far as we know) essential to its healthy functioning" (229). In an attempt "to supplement and guide the economic relation to land," Leopold suggests the image of a biotic pyramid. "The bottom layer is the soil," he writes, "a plant layer rests on the soil, an insect layer on the plants, a bird and rodent layer on the insects, and so on up through various animal groups to the apex layer, which consists of the larger carnivores" (230). This pyramid is also an energy circuit insofar as the plants absorb energy from the sun and that energy is circulated throughout the different layers. "Land, then, is not merely soil; it is a fountain of energy flowing through a circuit of soils, plants and animals" (231). Land is a community of life with humans occupying only one of the places at the table.

In Leopold's writing, the notion of land as community is juxtaposed to what he discerns as the prevailing attitude of land as adversary. Indeed he understands the choices facing humanity in quite stark terms: "man the conqueror *versus* man the biotic citizen; . . . land the slave and servant *versus* land the collective organism" (238).

Many things could be said about Leopold's essay and many things have been said by others. He was a professional forester, not a professional philosopher or ethicist, and professionals in these latter fields would want a more thorough elaboration of his position before they would count themselves persuaded (Callicott 1987). On the other hand there is something compelling about Leopold's position merely on the face of it. We do tend to treat the land as servant and slave and ourselves as conquerors. We are constantly demanding that the land release more and more of its fertility. We stand over it like Pharaoh over the Israelites constantly demanding more bricks with less straw. In pursuit of this goal we are demanding biological sacrifice in terms of whole species. To move from conqueror to citizen would be a shift worthy of the term revolutionary.

There are also problems with Leopold's position, even on its face. If we accept a community relationship with the land, is it obvious then, what the moral requirements are that flow from that relationship? In human community the norms for relationship have changed enormously over time. For example, in medieval Europe, people would have thought of themselves as being in community even though the pattern of those relationships were very hierarchical and substantively unequal. If we are going to be in community with the land, what are the social relationships that we are talking about?

In Christian circles, one of the most common metaphors used is the metaphor of stewardship. It is also easily and frequently employed by market oriented business writers. Humans are thought of, from this point of view, as holding the land, the natural world, in trust for God. Following from the creation myth as it is expounded in the book of Genesis, humans have been given dominion over the created world, which is understood as being different from domination.

> Then God said, "Let us make human beings in our image, after our likeness, to have dominion over the fish in the sea, the birds of the air, the cattle, all wild animals on land, and everything that creeps on the earth." Genesis 1: 26 (Revised English Bible)

It is a fiduciary responsibility we hold. We are made in the image of God, to act in God's place. We are to be good stewards of the earth. This image is repeated in the parables attributed to Jesus. A steward is a senior and trusted servant, and we are frequently exhorted to be "good and faithful servants" (see for example, Matt 24: 45–51 and Matt 25: 14–30). But while the image of trust is a positive one, the social relations being referred to are essentially ones of master and slave. We are being urged to be faithful servants in charge of possessions (things) or in charge of life forms that can't aspire to a position high enough up the hierarchy to qualify as senior servants themselves. This would seem to be exactly opposite to what Leopold was suggesting. He was arguing against an attitude that treated the land as "slave or servant."

This aspect of the Christian inheritance seems rarely attended to by Christians. As long as we only emphasize our understanding of dominion as meaning "caring for" and stewardship as "a trust relationship," the shadow side of these images as social relations will always be obscured. There is another image which is still widely used in agricultural circles which exposes the oppressive nature of our relationship to the land more clearly. This is an image and pattern which until very recently received unqualified support from the Christian churches but is now coming under increasing criticism. The image I'm referring to is the image of husbandry.

Contradictions in the Community of the Land

Husbandry is used by Aldo Leopold in the positive sense. He criticizes trophy hunters as being too immature to be good husbands and calls for a better appreciation of "husbandry-in-the-wild." What he is trying to convey is the importance of the "art of management" in relation to conservation (Leopold 1966: 267–268). But is this pattern of social relationships the pattern we want to promote in the community of the land? In this respect, stewardship and husbandry are very similar. Both attempt to communicate patterns of management, faithfulness, trusteeship and hierarchy. Both images lie at the core of what we call patriarchy.

The distinguished Canadian ecologist Stan Rowe recognizes this connection when he notes that while the term "husbandry" is becoming old-fashioned, the ideas behind it remain. "Read the sacred scriptures, study the works of the cultural giants, and an overpowering conclusion emerges. Only two relationships are important: that between Man and God, and that between Man and Man. The Man-Planet relationships is simply not recognized. . . . As an extension of what was expected in their homes, they projected an inert Nature, a passive Mother Earth, simply there to be *husbanded*. Today of course even husbandry is *passé*. We 'manage the resource base optimally' " (Rowe 1990: 29).

Some people suggest that patriarchy and husbandry are not accidentally connected. Elizabeth Fisher argues that since patriarchy as a social institution emerged at the same time as the domestication of animals, there must be a link. Perhaps the new knowledge of how animals procreate taught men about their own role as well. The conclusion drawn is that the forced mating of animals heralded the forced mating of women—rape (Fisher 1979).

Others disagree with this analysis. Gerda Lerner argues that patriarchy began as a functional division of labour and through a series of unanticipated developments turned into a system of oppression. She believes it possible that "the earliest sexual division of labour by which women *chose* occupations compatible with their mothering and child-raising activities were . . . acceptable to men and women alike" (Lerner 1986: 42). She cites examples of ancient societies where relatively egalitarian social structures co-existed with animal husbandry as evidence against the conclusions Fisher draws. She suggests rather that inter-tribal warfare in times of scarcity increased the power of warrior males (46), that the patterns of organisation demanded by grain agriculture reinforced the power of older, knowledgeable males (49) and that the strength required by plow agriculture diminished the power of pregnant and lactating females (51). She also points to the changes in ancient religious iconography where images of the goddess acquire a male consort but the female image is still dominant.[5]

It is not necessary for us to try and settle the argument about how and when patriarchy began. It is only necessary for us to recognize that husbandry understood as trusteeship or optimal management is a term that reflects a pattern of social relationship that is unequal and oppressive.[6] It is a pattern of relationship that produces violence against the community of women and violence against the community of the land.[7]

The positive dimension of the ancient and biblical view of husbandry is that it was an attempt to express the need for responsible, accountable caring for the community of the land. The negative aspect of husbandry is that this pattern of social relationship, within the context of market society, is experienced by those who are being husbanded as oppressive, demeaning and sometimes violent. It leads to death, not to life. If our current state is that we all live in a market society, and if we still want to practice responsible, accountable caring, our current question must become: What pattern of social relationship can furnish us with an adequate norm or ideal for the community? While some want to suggest an organic metaphor (see below) for this task, my own position is that this is incomplete and that we must supplant both mechanical (industrial) and organic metaphors for a relational metaphor. This means that the adequate norm for the community of the land is friendship.

From Mechanism to Organism to Relationship

Stan Rowe has identified our current problems with environmental degradation as the problems associated with an industrial approach to agriculture. The industrial approach to agriculture attempts to solve problems of scarcity through the application of the machine to the land for the sake of maximum production. It is based on a mechanistic view of the world. Rowe contrasts the mechanistic worldview with an ecological or organic worldview. "The organic and ecological view of Nature, as opposed to the mechanistic view," writes Rowe, "is religious in the true meaning of *religio*, to bind together, to make whole or holy." It is this latter worldview that will allow us to "return to the original goal of agriculture and, through it, the redemption of all culture" (1990: 174–175). I take this to be a version of the Romantic view which shares in the rich tradition of opposition to the Industrial Revolution of 200 years ago.[8] But because this view has been around awhile, we also know that the organic view has its limitations. One person who has thought a great deal about this is the Scottish philosopher, John Macmurray (1890–1976).[9]

Macmurray thought, "every period of human history is the embodiment of a philosophical idea" (1936:9). The period leading up to the Industrial Revolution was a period enthralled by the explanatory power of science, and science is based fundamentally on the manipulation of abstract symbols we call mathematical thought. According to Macmurray, mathematical thought represents all change as mechanical—that is, the object is thought of as passive and all change has an external cause. From this perspective, determinism and mechanism are the same thing. This type of approach represents the universe "as a mechanism in which all action is completely determined in accordance with causal laws. If such an interpretation is offered as a philosophy we have what is called 'materialism'" (98).

One limitation of this approach is that it only applies to things insofar as they are material. Mathematical thought, and therefore science, "arises from our interest in using things" and applies to things only insofar as they have utility. "That is why it issues in materialism"(100). That does not mean, however, that some things in the world are mechanically determined while others are not. Even this way of thinking, writes Macmurray, is a product of mechanical analysis. "*Everything* in the world is material. It may be that nothing in the world is merely material . . . . But organisms and persons, whatever more they may be, are certainly material objects" (101–102).The conclusion Macmurray draws from this is not that a mechanical approach to the world is invalid but rather that "it is valid for reality *in so far as it is material*"(102).

To the degree that reality also encompasses the immaterial, a mechanical approach will not be adequate. To the degree that reality is made up of life forms, we need to take a different approach, one that Macmurray describes as organic. What differentiates the biological world from the material world are the changes that are consistent within a given life form. We call these changes growth or development. Development is a process of change that moves an organism from a starting point through predictable and invariable stages to an end point. We can describe this process of change as a series of harmonious differences insofar as the end point which results is the end point which was intended from the start. We can call this a teleological approach if the *telos* or end is that which has been intended. So, we can say that the acorn contains within it the *telos* or end of the mature oak tree. This is not a matter of choice on the part of the acorn.

The limitation of this approach is that it cannot be adequate to describe life that is more than organic. Life insofar as it is organic adapts by responding to stimuli. Human life is more than merely organic and, while we do respond to stimuli, we are also capable of choosing our own ends, or telos. We are capable of being persons. The organic approach is an improvement over the mechanical approach, but if the community of the land is to include persons, we will need a third approach as well.

According to Macmurray, persons are individual human beings with a capacity for self-reflection which we call both consciousness and reason. Persons are individuals because, while they form groups, they are not completely subsumed by the group. They retain their own individual identity. We have the capacity to reflect on other persons, and through that, to reflect on ourselves and our own personality. Through this reflection we discover something unique. We experience that which is like us. We come to know our equal. Macmurray calls this the "consciousness of mutual relationship. . . . It is this essential mutuality which forms the essence of our experience of persons" (126).

Our capacity for self-reflection is also what we call reason because reason is the capacity for objectivity. By that Macmurray means that persons have the capacity "to stand in conscious relation to that which is recognized as not ourselves"(128). When two people are consciously relating to each other as persons in terms of their personality, we call that relationship friendship. When two persons are consciously relating to one another as master and slave, we say that the master is denying the full personhood of the slave. A person is being treated as a thing. When two people consciously relate to one another for the sake of a common purpose, the relationship is organic and teleological. Complete rationality, Macmurray suggests, can only be achieved within a relationship where people are consciously relating to one another *as persons*, that is to say, as friends. "The key to the nature of . . . reason, lies, then . . . in the nature of friendship"(134). If we are going to be interpreting the universe, we need to employ patterns of thought which do justice not only to the material world and the organic world but also to the personal world. Within the personal world, the norm for full rationality is represented by friendship.

Aldo Leopold identified the primary ecological problem as rooted in our industrial approach to agriculture. His response was to reframe our approach to the land. We are no longer dealing with the manipulation of the material world, we are now dealing with the social relations of a community. We also acknowledged, however, some limitations to Leopold's approach. Leopold employs patriarchal assumptions to govern the social relationships of the community. It is precisely the industrial approach to society that has exposed the inadequacy of the patriarchal approach. The social relations of market society have exposed themselves as violent and degrading to those without power—whether that means women or animals or soils. Stan Rowe and other ecologists who espouse romantic organicism share Leopold's anti-industrial approach but are themselves limited by treating the human participants in the community of the land in only their organic aspect. Macmurray suggests that his alternative metaphor of the personal relationship, which I am calling a relational approach, does justice to the human members of the community while allowing for the inclusion of both a material and organic approach. Further, since communities are defined by the active relationships of their members, a relational approach is more adequate for the community of the land. Finally, the moral norm that emerges from a relational approach is one of friendship. "Friendship," writes Macmurray, "is the essence of morality" (1932: 209).

Friendship as a Moral Norm

What's significant about friendship as a moral norm is that it presupposes freedom and describes a mutuality. It presupposes freedom in that I cannot be forced to be your friend. I must choose this quality of relationship for myself. I choose it not only because I stand to gain from it but because I genuinely care for the other person. In Macmurray's terms, communities are based on "positive personal motivation" (1961: 146). Friendship does not require material equality. The parties to the relationship don't have to be the same in all their aspects. They do have to be the same, however, at the level of respect. A poor person can be friends with a rich person, a woman with a man, an American with a German, and a sighted person with someone who is blind. This is an important feature if we are going to apply this metaphor to the community of the land.

Some people might argue that we cannot be friends to the land because the soils, plants and animals are not able to be friends in return. I don't agree. When we talk about being friends, we are talking about choosing a quality of relationship insofar as we are able. Not sharing the same language will be a limitation on our relationship but it does not mean we cannot be in relationship at all. It doesn't mean we can't be friends. Friendship as a model for the community of the land evokes the same images of caring and respect that both Leopold and Rowe desire. "Agri/culture means the cultivation of fields to produce crops. Within the words *culture* and *cultivation* is *cultus*, to care. Behind it, in turn, is the Sanskrit word *kwei* meaning to dwell with, as well as to care for. We are led back to an idea, deep in the language, that agriculture has to do with people dwelling on the land and caring for it" (Rowe 1990: 166). It also embodies the positive attitudes that Wendell Berry calls for. "To have community," Berry writes, "people don't need a 'community centre.' . . . Instead they need to love each other, trust each other, and help each other" (Berry 1987: 176).

Some people will judge the ethics of our agricultural practice not by our duties to the land nor even by our intentions. Rather, they will judge the morality of our practice by its consequences. They will want to know how a morality of friendship within the community of the land would make a difference. A morality of friendship is not a morality of domination. If friends do not support one another they are not friends. When they are in trouble, friends stand in solidarity with one another. They empower one another. A morality of friendship is not indifferent to the loss of biodiversity nor to the destruction of habitat for our neighbours whether they are geese or deer or worms or farmers. Friendship is typified by caring and compassion—a genuine interest and concern for the well-being of the other. A morality of friendship seeks life in abundance for the friend (Gen. 1:28), but it does not worship at the altar of production. A true friend does not promote a life of chemical dependency in order to cope with living. When the community is in trouble, friends come to each other's aid. If our agricultural practice were governed by a morality of friendship today, we would be organising a massive campaign to redevelop and repopulate the countryside. As Wendell Berry put it, "One of the meanings of our current high rates of soil erosion is that we do not have enough farmers; we have enough farmers to use the land but not enough to use it and protect it at the same time" (1987: 164). But we would be repopulating not only the human members of the community but all the members of the community. If our friends could speak our language, is this not what they would say to us?

Conclusion

Stan Rowe describes the choice before us as a choice between "tinkering" and "transforming." "The tinkerers advocate conservation tillage, meaning such changes as snow management to increase the effectiveness of precipitation, the addition of phosphorous and nitrogen to the soil through formulated fertilizers, the greater use of rotations and leguminous nitrogen-fixing crops and substituting chemical poisoning for mechanical weeding—subtle violence for overt violence— to slow soil deterioration. Such techniques buy time and extend the life of conventional agriculture, but they are not the long-term solution"(1990: 183).

"The transformers advocate low-input farming, accenting the organic nature of healthy soil and good food. . . . They judge each agricultural technique according to whether it helps or hinders human participation in the world's renewing processes. . . . Agro-ecosystems must be designed to meet the expectations of the Ecosphere, the capabilities of the land, and not just those of the people in and on it" (184).

The Senate Report called for a revolution in our agricultural practice. I have tried to show in this chapter that the conditions that give rise to that call have not diminished but have gotten worse. I have also tried to show how it could be that the environmental crisis is one of the many crises that combine to form what we call the farm crisis in Saskatchewan. Finally, I have tried to show that the unity of thought and practice that has produced the environmental crisis is itself generated out of the moral economy of market society. The farmers involved in farm protest have identified powerlessness as a major feature of this form of social organisation. They have also linked the survival of the environment to the survival of human community. Because I accept Leopold's call for us to recognize our membership in the community of the land, I am calling in turn for a new moral economy based on the norms of friendship. Only friendship can serve as an ideal for a responsible, accountable caring that is not degrading or violent. The norm of friendship can generate a policy of repopulation for both organic and human members of the community. It tinkers neither with patriarchy nor with industrial agriculture. It represents a true transformation.

Notes

1. Fertilizer use as measured by sales figures increased from $11.5 million in 1971 to $253.3 million in 1989. Pesticide figures include sales of herbicides. These farm chemicals increased from $7 million in 1971 to $234 million in 1989. In order to discount the impact of inflation these figures have been multiplied by the Farm Input Price Index giving figures in constant 1986 dollars. The adjusted figures indicate that fertilizer sales increased from an equivalent of $36.7 million to $233.7 million and pesticide and herbicide sales increased from an equivalent of $22.4 million to $216.5 million between 1971 and 1989. Raw data came from Statistics Canada.

2. "Low commodity prices and high input costs have also pushed farmers to continuously increase yields—simply to remain financially afloat" (Sparrow 1984: 17).
3. It should also be noted that the Task Force anticipated needing to put social supports in place for farm families in poverty and recommended a form of the Guaranteed Annual Income or negative Income Tax. This approach to poverty was being actively debated in government circles at the time but was dropped from the government agenda in the mid 1970s. See p. 425 of the Report.
4. See also Porter 1990. Following the publication of his book, Porter was hired by the Canadian government to do a study of competitiveness in the Canadian economy.
5. "With the establishment of husbandry and the domestication of flocks and herds, however, the function of the male in the process of generation became more apparent and vital as the physiological facts concerning paternity were more clearly understood and recognized. Then the mother-goddess was assigned a male partner, either in the capacity of her son and lover, or of brother and husband. Nevertheless, although he was the begetter of life he occupied a subordinate position to her, being in fact a secondary figure in the cultus" (Lerner 1986: 228). See also James 1959.
6. For an example of Christian ethical reflection on patriarchy see Fiorenza 1985.
7. For examples of Christian ethical reflection on the connections between patriarchy and violence against women see Lebacqz 1980 and Moore 1980.
8. The environmental movement is rooted in a Romantic approach, according to Peter Timmerman 1990.
9. John Macmurray is most well known today for his Gifford Lectures of 1953/54 which were published in two volumes in 1956 and 1961, though in his own time he had a much wider and popular following. I am turning to Macmurray because of his elaboration of three styles of thought or worldviews, which he described as mechanical, organic and personal. He elaborated these ideas most fully in his 1936 volume.

CHAPTER FOUR

Building Community
as a Response to Globalization

Rural Dignity

I never knew my grandmother but I can easily imagine that she looked a lot like Barb Bonneau. When I first saw Barb she was seated behind a table in the hallway outside a hotel conference room. She has warm grey hair curled close to her head and a gentle, inviting smile. Hanging on the wall behind her was a handmade quilt. She could have been tending the bake table at a church tea. Instead, she was distributing pamphlets on behalf of Rural Dignity—a populist protest and action group campaigning to save Canada's rural post offices. Barb's been the president since 1988.

The quilt was a protest banner made in folk art style. The protests began in 1986 after the Tory government of Brian Mulroney began to close the rural post offices. The campaign was entitled, "Coast to Coast for Rural Post." Barb was patient as she told me the story she's probably told a hundred times before. There are 5,200 rural post offices representing about 10,000 jobs. When the post offices are eliminated from small towns, the jobs are lost, the income is lost and the only federal building in town is closed. But that's not the end of the story. The other effects are more elusive but just as damaging.

When the post office is closed, rural residents are offered three choices: bad, worse, and terrible. A postal counter will be established in a local store, a clump of "lock-boxes" will be built in town, or residents can drive to the next nearest centre with postal service. (These forced choices remind me of the lay minister from southern Saskatchewan I met in 1989. She told me that in the last ten years her address had changed three time but she still hadn't moved!) When a small town only has two grocery stores, the location of a postal counter in one of them establishes a new level of harsh competition. Rural stores often carry customers on credit, and they can't afford to have their customer base eroded even further. The community is divided along loyalty versus convenience lines, and the non-postal store will finally close—another service, income, and employment opportunity gone.

If it were up to the communities, there would be open-ended discussion about how the rural postal service should be run. The community members would be consulted about hours and in some small locations people could volunteer their time to keep it open. Other government services (provincial and municipal as well as federal) would be encouraged to use the postal building. Barb was getting more and more animated as she pointed out that profit and loss weren't the main issues in rural postal service. She described how the post office became a Crown Corporation in 1981 and that a commission headed by Senator Marchand (the ex-labour leader, Trudeau ally, and wise man from the East) found rural service to be only marginally related to the profit and loss problem of the post office. The main business of the postal service now is not service at all but direct-mail advertising. It seems every move that Canada Post now makes is a move away from rural Canada. How long before rural delivery routes will be privatized and how long after that before the deliveries become less frequent in order to become more profitable?

I knew about the loss of the postal subsidy to Canadian magazines but I had not stopped to think about the implications of these cuts for rural newspapers. Indeed, this was a significant cost increase for rural newspapers, most of whose subscribers receive the newspaper by mail. Barb Bonneau's concern was the elimination of independent publications which provide alternative and local points of view.

She continued her description of the impact of rural post office closings. Most rural post offices have photocopiers and they're typically the only public photocopiers in town. Most rural postmasters and postmistresses are also notaries public, serving to witness legal documents and oaths. These ancillary services could have been expanded. The local buildings are not actually owned by Canada Post. They're owned by Canada Works. People are proud of these facilities; it means a lot to rural Canadians to have the Canadian flag flying in their town.

I interrupted the Rural Dignity president because I wanted to know more about the significance of the term "dignity" in the group's name. This had obviously been the topic of other conversations. There was a defensive edge in her voice.

"There's nothing dignified about being impoverished," she said. "There's no freedom to poverty. What we're doing is fighting for rural people to maintain their dignity. We want to let other people know there is great dignity in rural Canada." It had become clear to me that this group was protesting the series of indignities being inflicted on rural Canada from all sources. It could have been the railways that caught their venom. It happened to be the post office. In either case, the federal government was being held to account for it.

From their point of view it was government policies that were causing a lot of the problems. "Government policies are making the market effects worse," she said. "They're implementing policies that breakdown the infrastructure." The feelings of abandonment and betrayal were thick in the space around us. The most fundamental assumptions about Canadian identity and Canadian history were now being questioned. "Are we being told that generations of people made the wrong choice to live in rural Canada?"

Barb Bonneau's quilt and the name of the organisation, Rural Dignity, speak eloquently to the perspective and feelings of rural Canadians. People living outside the great metropolitan areas and involved in agriculture and other forms of primary production experience broken relationships with their fellow citizens. Relationships of trust, cooperation, reciprocity and respect have been sundered. The dignity of their community has been assaulted. Their personhood has been violated.

In the introduction to this book, I identified cooperation and community as one of the moral categories used by farmers to explain their frustration. It is also one of the basepoints for their protest against the current crisis. Farmers experience a crisis in every form and level of their communities. At the most intimate level farm wives see their husbands being destroyed. "We're tired of seeing our husbands grow old before their time." At a social level they realise they need to re-establish older patterns of cooperation in order to survive. "We need to get together or we'll all be gone."[1]

In the first chapter, I explained how globalization lies at the heart of the current crisis. It is not the only problem but it is the single most important factor which distinguishes this crisis from other farm crises. It is the change which unites the farm crisis with the fisheries crisis, with the manufacturing crisis, and with the jobs crisis. As I explained in chapter three, when a society is faced with a systematic change of this magnitude, some people want to bless the change and promote policies designed to accommodate shifts in the structure. Others resist.

How is resistance possible? Some resist simply by trying to organise against change. I sympathize with this approach but I also think it is limited. A more successful strategy is to build a base for a different future. The way to do that is very old fashioned. We do that by building community.

What is community?

In the 1950s, G. Hillery undertook an analysis of ninety-four different definitions of community. The greatest areas of agreement in these definitions involved the possession of common ends, norms, or means (1955). Many people associate community with place or geographic locale. In this sense, my community is the place from which I come. However, contemporary changes in transportation and communication have revealed the inadequacy of that criterion. In a stable population, people in a given locale have similar interests and needs relative to the larger population away from that place. The normal activities of daily living bring individuals into regular communication with one another so that common objectives can be achieved and conflicts resolved. Over time this creates a shared history and eventually a shared identity.

However, in an age of telecommunications where a population is mobile, it is possible for people to be living in different places and yet share and pursue common objectives through regular communication. They may belong to a community without sharing a place. It is the difference between belonging and residing.

The difference between belonging and residing has another parallel in the difference between being and belonging. One can belong to an association but real community is part of who you are.[2] It is part of your social being. This distinction was advanced in the 1920s by R. M. McIver who described community as "the common life of social being" (McIver 1924, quoted in Roberts 1979: 31). This is a more adequate approach for our purposes since it includes the sense of intimacy and identity found in the concept articulated by farmers. When farmers protest that their communities are at stake, they do not only mean the economic viability of the nearest town. They are also referring to the quality of relationship. Those relationships are becoming less equal, less free, and less personal. "We can no longer work like slaves and work more and more for less and less." There is less opportunity for sharing, caring, and mutual support. "We lash out at those nearest—our families."

Another reason we associate community with place is because we associate shared histories, identities, and mutual support with pre-industrial culture. This image is especially strong in agricultural areas. In spite of the fact that modern farming would be almost unrecognizable to a nineteenth-century farmer, the immobility of farm land and the intergenerational employment patterns among farmers continue to provide the infrastructure, the material reality, that is the pre-requisite for community, just as it was before the Industrial Revolution.

This dividing line was employed by the German sociologist, Ferdinand Tœnnies in his book, *Community and Society*. In that book he was able to capture the spirit of the transition to industrial European culture by contrasting community (*gemeinschaft*) with society (*gesellschaft*). He described community as private and intimate, but also as exclusive and organic. It was closed to strangers and developed according to its own logic.

Society, on the other hand, he associated with modernity. It was the result of free association and contract. It was urban if not cosmopolitan, and very public. It was the product of rational will. The contrast between intimate relationships and public associations is very similar to McIver. Though Tœnnies was able to capture the nineteenth-century romantic longing for the past, clearly in the march of human progress, community was to be supplanted by society. What he was unable to grasp was that community was capable of being realized intentionally, albeit indirectly. In that sense, what is missing from Tœnnies' definition is an understanding of freedom appropriate to persons.

In chapter three we introduced the work of the philosopher John Macmurray, for whom the concept of community was central. Like Macmurray I reserve the term community to describe personal relationships which involve history, identity, mutuality, and fellowship. Following Tœnnies and MacIver, most of what passes for community in common parlance is really association or society. So, a community of teachers is more helpfully described as a society of teachers since the relationships are pragmatic, not personal. Even so, within the society a variety of communities may develop, all of which are comprised exclusively of teachers. As Macmurray put it, "Every community is then a society; but not every society is a community" (1961: 146).

In a more recent and more fully developed theory of community, Philip Selznick affirms the shift from location to quality of relationship but expands the list of characteristics that need to be present. "Any theory we propose must take into account the key values at stake in the construction and nurture of a community. These constitute a complex set of interacting variables: historicity, identity, mutuality, plurality, autonomy, participation, and integration" (1992: 361). For Selznick, community is a *prima facie* good thing. Like culture, friendship, socialization, and family life, "Communities provide settings within which people grow and flourish and within which subgroups are nourished and protected. This establishes a presumption of moral worth" (Selznick 1992: 360).

Like Macmurray, Selznick sees community as a quality of relationship which is essential to full human personhood. It involves more than the reciprocity of shared interests. It involves a concern for the other we describe as mutuality. "As we move to association, and from association to community, mutuality reaches beyond exchange to create more enduring bonds of interdependence, caring, and commitment. There is a transition, we may say, from reciprocity to solidarity, and from there to fellowship" (360).

In his inclusion of the distinction between association and community, Selznick goes beyond other writers in reserving a role for organisations. Indeed, as a process, Selznick describes a progression from organisation to institution to community. "A sense of institutional identity and an ideal of community are most likely to develop where values are more central than goals or at least are equally important, and where goals are multiplied in order to accommodate a broad range of interests. The formula "organization —> institution —> community" applies most clearly (but also variably) to schools, universities, hospitals, churches, professional associations, advocacy groups, political parties, and government agencies. The narrower and more instrumental the animating purpose, the more resistance there will be to thick institutionalization and the claims of community"

(237–238). Selznick's understanding that community requires institutions will be important as we try and understand how community has been eroded and how it can be rebuilt.

How has globalization eroded community?

If we want to build community in the context of globalization, we need to understand the mechanism by which globalization erodes community. That mechanism will have to be reversed. Let us review the process of globalization.

In the first instance globalization refers to a concrete "material change." It refers to the linking of national markets for financial capital to form one global capital market. The most dramatic changes occured between 1971 and 1979. The process was made possible through the technological innovation of the microchip. The microchip made computers possible and computers made possible the instantaneous transfer of currency around the world.

This material change had the effect of "shifting power" away from political voices and social institutions and toward economic voices and market institutions. For example, in the 1960s, the Bank of Canada operated on the assumption that it controlled interest rates in Canada and exchange rates for the Canadian currency. Now, in the 1990s the Bank of Canada operates on the assumption that it doesn't control either, but that it can speed up or slow down the rate of change. Though some may argue that the latter is the real truth and the former was always mistaken, it seems entirely possible that both statements could be true in their own time. When finance capital was moving within a market defined by specific political boundaries, it was possible for an institution within those boundaries to effectively regulate that market. When the boundaries of the market became massively larger than the boundaries of the nation, power shifted from the nation to the market. Instead of the Bank of Canada regulating the market, the market now regulates the Bank of Canada.

This power shift created a practical dilemma. The world environment was changing rapidly, before everyone really knew what was going on or what the implications were. People were now operating on the basis of ideas which no longer corresponded to the material reality. The social structure was also reflective of and defended by these same ideas. What emerged was a "battle of ideas." Some people are taking the material change as a positive occurence. They seek to reform our social structure to harmonize with the new reality. They preach efficiency and competitiveness in the new global marketplace. By advocating that these economic criteria be applied to social institutions like schools, hospitals, and social welfare agencies, they are advocating the priority of the market over society, of economics over politics.

On the other hand, we also hear voices describing the new material reality as a negative development. These people seek to defend themselves against the losses which result from diminished political control of economic activity. They seek to resist the unregulated expansion of transnational capital. Against the efficiency of the market mechanism is placed the justice of democratic decision-making. This ideological struggle is waged over the conscience of society. What hangs in the balance is our attitude, which conditions our action, which effects our ethics. It is an ideological struggle because it is a battle of ideas. It is a moral struggle because it is a dispute about what constitutes "good" social policy.

Insofar as the proponents of globalization have been successful, their approach has framed the public policy agenda. President Reagan and Prime Minister Mulroney were both proponents of globalization. Their agenda was known as a neo-conservative one because it endorsed the benefits of market-driven social change. Their legacy to us is the North American Free Trade Agreement (NAFTA). Neither President Clinton nor Prime Minister Chretien were known as neo-conservatives and both represent political parties opposed to the previous regimes. However, since the policies of both governments have been focussed on "restructuring" the state (government and its agencies) they both, in practice, can be located "within the neo-conservative agenda which seeks to bless globalization." In the process of restructuring, market forces and market institutions are given moral and political priority. This means that services previously organised and delivered by government (like health care) are "privatized" (delivered by private agencies who bid on contracts in the market place). It also means that activities previously regulated by the state (barley marketing through the Canadian Wheat Board, for example) are thought to be better handled by the market. The moral priority of one approach is supplanted by the economic priority of the other.

What has just been described is a four stage process. First there was a change in the material reality which produced a power shift. This power shift weakened key institutions resulting in a battle of ideas followed by a government initiated restructuring of other institutions. In order to understand how this four-stage process destroys community, we need to return to our discussion of community.

Macmurray argued that communities were different from associations because the latter were pragmatic and the former were personal. Selznick linked community with institutions and organisations. Essentially when people first come together (associate), they form organisations around shared interests. These organisations develop institutions if their needs are sustained over time. It is in the context of the ongoing life of institutions that people come to care about one another as persons and communities are born. For Selznick, institutions are central. "Institutions embody values and enhance integration, but they do so in ways that resist homogeneity and sustain differentiation. Strong communities are *institution-centered*" (370). This persistent effort to distinguish community from association and yet describe their interrelationships has other implications as well. The "discussion of plurality and distinction between community and association is really a plea for the institutions of civil society and the distinction between community and society" (362–363).

What is civil society?

The study of society and community is a field dominated by sociologists and political scientists. The latter group of scholars use a term which has become increasingly important in recent years. The term is civil society. Prior to the nineteenth century, this term, *societas civilis,* referred only to political society and therefore, the state (Bobbio 1979: 26). The philosopher G.W.F. Hegel gave this term a new meaning.

> As a result of Hegel's view many political theorists now distinguish "civil society" from "state," using the first to denote forms of association which are spontaneous, customary, and in general not dependent on law, and the second to denote the legal and political institutions which protect, endorse, and bring to completion the powerful but inarticulate forces of social union. (Scruton 1983: 66)

For Hegel, the term "civil society" replaced what other theorists referred to as "natural society," meaning that intermediate set of social relationships between the family and the state. In modern use it tends to include even family relationships.

Though marxists tended to see civil society as another aspect of the state, it was a twentieth century Italian marxist, Antonio Gramsci, who rehabilitated the concept by returning to Hegel's understanding of it. Gramsci argued that civil society was not merely a reflection of the power of existing elites but rather an independent arena of ethical action (Bobbio 1979: 31). Though operating within constraints, the clubs, associations, churches, schools, unions, and other groups that constitute civil society were areas of authentic freedom. In order for fundamental changes to occur peacefully within a society, the leading element in society had to exercise leadership (hegemony) within the arena of civil society.

> Once the moment of civil society is considered as the moment in which the transition from necessity to freedom takes place, the ideologies, which have their historical roots in civil society, are no longer seen just as a posthumous justification of a power which has been formed historically by material conditions, but are seen as forces capable of creating a new history and of collaborating in the formation of a new power, rather than to justify a power which has already been established. (36)

Gramsci's use of Hegel's concept was novel, but what he has argued is that there is another place in society where the struggle for social change takes place. It's not on the shop floor of Marx's revolutionary workplace and it's not in the legislative assembly of John Locke's liberal state. It's in the regular meetings of everyone's local, voluntary organisation—the place where community is formed.

Ironically, the best illustration that Gramsci gave of what civil society looked like was the Christian church in the middle ages. In that period of time he understood the church to be

> the hegemonic apparatus of the ruling group. For the latter did not have its own apparatus, i.e., did not have its own cultural and intellectual organisation, but regarded the universal, ecclesiastical organisation as being that. (Gramsci, Prison Notebooks, quoted in Bobbio 1979: 30)

How can we build community?

We have described community in personal rather than geographic terms, but relationships do not exist and are not created out of thin air. In political economic terms, they require a material reality. In theological terms they need to be incarnate. While they may include warm feelings they need to be made of flesh and blood. The most intimate form of community is a family. Not all families form community (some can be quite destructive) but when a group of biological strangers form community they are said to be like family to one another.[3]

A community has a shared history and shared histories are created by common action. In common action intentions are formed and fulfilled; visions are realized. A community has a shared identity. A shared identity is acquired through the articulation, adaptation, and affirmation of shared values. These intentions, visions, and values are worked out in the context of other activities. If community is to be formed, people must be willing to cooperate for a common purpose. In the course of working out the purpose, community may be formed. Frank Kirkpatrick puts it this way:

> Cooperation may, in fact, prove to be a catalyst for the discovery of the joy of fellowship but it is not, in and of itself, a substitute for it. For example, workers may cooperate so closely in a common economic task that they begin to experience a commonality of interests. Out of that interest they might form a union whose primary objective is to secure the practical realization of their common economic concern. But derivatively, out of the union experience may eventually come the experience of delight simply in being together. Now this latter experience is not the original function of the union nor its primary purpose, but it may arise out of the conditions of association provided by its function. (1986: 211)

If cooperation will not necessarily result in community it is certainly a precondition for it. In order for cooperation to occur there must be an actual pattern of activity, an action, a material reality to give it life.

> If the members of the mutual/personal community have as their overarching intention to enjoy fellowship with each other, then there must be material conditions which both prepare for the possibility of that intention and enable it to be carried out in practice. In other words, a mutual intentionality for community requires material conditions and infrastructures which are subordinate to but essential aspects of the full realization of that intentionality. (Kirkpatrick 1986: 206)

Globalization erodes community by changing the material reality that communities rely on as a framework for their common action. The consequent power shift away from the nation state and towards global capital creates benefits for transnational corporations and costs for national governments. It strengthens the power of an unregulated global capital market and weakens the power of financial institutions (like the Bank of Canada) accountable to democratic governments. There is currently a battle of ideas being waged in civil society. The ideas that are currently dominant trumpet the values of a transient, urban labour force which is newly competitive in a global market which has been freed from regulation by a much smaller government working within the constraints of balanced budgets. To the extent that these forces have had their effect, community has been further eroded by governments that restructure by eliminating or reducing the agencies or programs in which communities used to find shelter. As was indicated earlier, because community is not accidental it can be realised intentionally. The way to fight globalization is by intentionally building community. The way to build community is by reversing the process of erosion.

As the process of globalization has been analyzed in these pages, the most recent attack on community has come from the restructuring efforts of our own governments. The appropriate response to a government of restructuring is a "politics of resistance." The aim of this kind of political activity is to slow down or stop the erosion. Shelters from the storm of market forces have been built up slowly and painstakingly over many generations. They can be torn down with surprising speed. Some market-oriented governments liken themselves to medical practitioners with a necessary but unwelcome task. They can remove the bandage from the gaping wound slowly or quickly. They invariably choose the latter and congratulate themselves for it. More time is needed to facilitate the building of new and stronger shelters.

The politics of resistance goes hand in hand with a "struggle for the conscience of society." This involves a redeployment of resources in the ethical arena of civil society. Globalization is a powerful concept because it draws its strength from a powerful reality. "Ordinary people," farmers and other citizens, do not feel empowered to resist globalization because it does not seem like something within their control. All of these people belong to organisations that could say no. The elevation of competitiveness as the only criteria by which society should be judged can only occur with the quiet assent of ordinary people meeting in town halls, church basements, and coffee shops. This is where the ideology of competitiveness will receive its patriarchal blessing. In the humble act of dissent lies the power of democratic freedom.

The struggle for the conscience of society has two moments. In the first moment, ordinary people can reclaim their freedom by saying no to the ethics of globalization. In saying no to competitiveness, they are also saying no to domination of their neighbour and refusing to be indifferent to the strangers in their midst. In the second moment, they must say yes. They must say yes to their own history of cooperation for the common good. They must say yes to the challenges of solidarity with people who are suffering injustice, and they must say yes to the call to compassion.

Just as it is not easy to claim one's own freedom, even when it has been there for the taking all the time, so it is not easy to stand in solidarity with strangers, foreigners, competitors, and others with whom one is not yet in community. It is risky. It is dangerous. It requires faith in a common humanity. It requires the support of others. There is no step we can take short of doing it. For this reason we need to consider a strategy which is consistent with the goal. In the second moment, we must be willing to form democratic coalitions across previous divisions for the sake of intentionally building community. They must be coalitions because we need new allies in this struggle and because we cannot be in solidarity without acting in solidarity. They must be democratic because only democratic organisations can foster the liberty and equality necessary for community.

The purpose of the democratic coalitions is to redesign or rebuild "new institutions." The unregulated market is a powerful and potentially destructive force. By itself it is amoral. It has no conscience. If it were human we would say that it is sociopathic and incarcerate it as a danger to other humans. Instead we worship at its feet. Our existing institutions were built on the basis of certain assumptions, like the power of central banks to regulate exchange rates. Some of these institutions will need to be refashioned on the basis of revised assumptions. Some do not yet exist and will need to be invented. Others will need to be made responsive to the wishes of citizens. These new and changed institutions will provide the material reality we require for the communities we intend to build. Globalization has produced its own new institutions like NAFTA. Given the power wielded by these institutions we should be shocked that they don't bare any of the hallmarks of representative democracy.

The net effect of forming democratic coalitions for the purpose of building new institutions is to "extend democracy" to the economic sphere. Globalization has once more ripped economic forces from their embeddedness in the political structure of nation states and inverted the relationship between politics and economics. To the extent that nation states are democratic, ordinary people now have less control over economic forces than they did before, and the market now has much more control over our politics than it ever did.

By democracy I do not mean a quadrennial exercise of casting one's ballot as a choice between competing choices. By democracy I mean the right of people to participate in decisions which affect them. Some of the most powerful decisions being made about our lives today are being made through the decentralized mechanism of a global market without any democratic reference to the people most affected by the outcomes. In order to achieve that reference we need to discover a new political and social framework in which we can re-embed the global market. Only then will a democratic reference truly be possible.

The extension of democracy will be the last step in realising the intention of building community. In order for community to be fully community, it must create not only a shared history and identity but also a quality of relationship we call mutuality. For a relationship to be mutual it must be freely entered into. There can be no coercion or force. Also for it to be mutual, one person must regard the other as they regard themselves. They must regard them as an equal—neither superior nor subordinate regardless of any differences in abilities or characteristics. This is what John Macmurray meant when he wrote: "Thus equality and freedom are constitutive of community; and the democratic slogan, 'Liberty, equality, fraternity,' is an adequate definition of community—of the self-realization of persons in relation" (1961: 158).

Not only is democracy central to the building of community but the building of community is also central to strong democratic theory.

> Far from positing community *a priori*, strong democratic theory understands the creation of community as one of the chief tasks of political activity in the participatory mode. Far from positing historical identity as the condition of politics, it posits politics as the conditioner of given historical identities—as the means by which men are emancipated from determinative historical forces (Barber, quoted in Selznick 1992: 523–524).

So this is how community is built—intentionally, yet indirectly. The forces eroding community are slowed down or stopped altogether. The struggle for the conscience of society is engaged at the level of civil society where ordinary citizens have the opportunity to say no to the ideology of competitiveness and yes to the ethic of compassion and solidarity. Democratic coalitions are formed in order to build and rebuild new institutions to serve the common good. In the end, the market is re-embedded and democracy is extended so that people have secure access to the power they need to participate in the decisions which effect them.

A Case Study in Building Community

Farmers in Saskatchewan have been losing their land at an unprecedented rate. There is no section of the province that is unaffected. As of January 1993 over 14,000 farmers in Saskatchewan alone had been through either a provincial or federal farm debt review process. This represents 23 percent of all farmers in the province and does not include a further 14,822 dependents affected by the farm debt review process. In at least four rural municipalities over 50 percent of the farmers have been through this process.

For people with a personal experience of this kind of community trauma, the possibility of forming democratic coalitions to build new institutions may seem too remote to be real. For that reason, I want to use the question of land tenure as a case study in building community. I suggested that the first step in intentionally building community was to engage in the politics of resistance. In the context of farmers losing their land, that means "resisting the market-driven policies of elected officials or changing the governments." In Saskatchewan in 1994, the most ideologically pro-market government in sixty years has already been defeated so it now means resisting the policies of a government confused about its current direction. In Alberta, the populace recently elected a determinedly pro-market government so the resistance there will need to be more electoral. Of course, there are many levels of government. Sometimes it is possible to use the resources of municipal governments to resist the policies of provincial or federal governments.

The politics of resistance can also be a way to mobilize people and to build the democratic coalitions necessary for the second stage. People in farm communities and members of community organisations need to support each other. For example, I have reflected elsewhere on the role of the churches in the farm crisis (Lind 1992). Among other suggestions I recommended that members of congregations publicly declare their intention to ensure that no one has to go through the farm debt review process alone. This is not because Christians have any special expertise in farm land security legislation but because one of our greatest hurdles to overcome is our tendency to treat farm finance as a "private" matter between farmer and lender. If a church member accompanies a farmer to a meeting with the bank, then just by being present and witnessing the proceedings they have made the affairs "public" and open to scrutiny. Such acts of solidarity become the building blocks of the democratic coalitions we require. They make the business of food production everybody's business.

Not everybody who goes through the farm debt review process ends up losing their land but the largest percentage of cases end up with a "quit claim and lease back." The farmer gives up title to the land and becomes a renter of that same land, now owned by the financial institution. One of the longterm consequences of this process is that the Farm Credit Corporation (FCC), a federal institution, has become the largest land owner in the province with over a million acres of farm land. One of the goals of a democratic coalition might be to "ensure that this FCC land is not sold until other alternative tenure arrangements have been explored."

The forming of coalitions is part of the struggle for the conscience of society. The crisis in land ownership is a sign of massive market failure in agriculture. Parents cannot pass farm land on to the next generation and young farmers without farming parents cannot afford to borrow the money needed to buy a whole operation. Will we have a clear conscience about this new "clearance" of people from the land, or will we acknowledge our shame at this collective failure and struggle together to build something new? A coalition to stop the sale of FCC land and explore alternatives can be one way to challenge everyone's conscience.

The third step in our intentional efforts to build community in response to globalization is to redesign and rebuild more appropriate institutions in which to have our social life. In this case it means "renovating or rebuilding alternatives to the land tenure institution." Such a proposal must face immediate skepticism. Farmers in Saskatchewan are fiercely attached to the private ownership of land. Perhaps it is because for many European families near the turn of the century, it was the first time their families had ever owned land. As one woman put it to me:

> I grew up on a farm. My parents were farmers. My grandparents were farmers. They were farmers in Ireland before they came over. Their parents were farmers and their parents were farmers and so on as far back as we can trace. When my grandparents homesteaded in Saskatchewan, they were the first generation to ever have title to their land.

Of course, the liberation of a landless European class came at the price of the dispossession of the First Nations of the area.[4] Ironically, this is important now because the settlement of land claims in the province means new financial resources will be available for the purchase of farm land. Band councils with capital to invest in farming will be natural allies in attempts to build new institutions.

In the 1970s the Saskatchewan government created a land bank. The purpose of the land bank was to facilitate the transfer of farm land between generations and the entry into farming of a new generation without access to family holdings. This land would always belong to the land bank and would not need to be refinanced with each generation. The land bank stopped acquiring new land in 1984 under a new pro-market government. Opinion among farmers is divided about how the land bank was administered but it appears to have been successful in its specific goals.[5]

In light of that recent experience, a new proposal has been developed for a land trust. Following a model used in the United States to protect environmentally sensitive areas, this proposal involves establishing a corporation with a local board which would raise capital through the sale of bonds. The farmer would have the exclusive right to farm the land and to pass the land on to the next generation but title would be held by the trust and an income paid by the farmer to the bond holders (see Brown 1992). There have also been proposals circulating for a land cooperative arrangement (see Bendel et al. 1992).

Each of these are examples of the creativity available in the province for the development of alternative institutions. They are also examples of the development of coalitions. The land trust proposal, for example, was sponsored by several churches, the credit union movement and Federated Cooperatives, and the Saskatchewan Wheat Pool.

The last step in the framework of intentionally building community as a response to globalization is the extension of democracy. In the context of a struggle over land tenure this means forging links with other groups in other areas of the economy and other groups in other provinces to increase people's ability to participate in decisions which effect them. Our ancestors knew about this last step. They were not content with the establishment of the Canadian Wheat Board, local credit unions, or local cooperatives. They also worked to establish an institution—the Cooperative College—where the principles of cooperation could be studied and taught. Links were made with international agencies so the benefits of cooperation could be shared.

In this generation though, some of those institutions have been closed. Some co-ops present themselves as one more option in the marketplace rather than an alternative to market domination. The next generation is no longer being nurtured with the vision of a different future. Globalization is not a phenomenon unique to Saskatchewan or even to agriculture. All over the world people are being buffeted by exactly the same forces. They are being forced away from traditional activities toward market activities. Control is shifting away from communities and toward capital and markets. That is why the intentional building of communities

Ethics of Globalization and Community

Competition	**Ethic**	Cooperation	*Goal*	Community
Domination	**Activity**	Solidarity	*Strategy*	Coalitions
Indifference	**Attitude**	Compassion	*Approach*	Democratic

is the appropriate response not only to the farm crisis in Saskatchewan but to the financial revolution called globalization. Recalling how the ethics of globalization were charted in chapter three, we can see how the response of building community fits in the diagram which follows.

The task of building community as a response to globalization is a task not only for us but for the whole world. Our allies are waiting.

Notes

1. Comments made at the Rosetown Rally.
2. Michael Sandel summed it up this way: "For them, community describes not just what they *have* as fellow citizens but also who they *are*, not a relationship they choose (as in a voluntary association) but an attachment they discover, not merely an attribute but a constituent of their identity" (1982: 150).
3. For other practical ideas on how to build community see Nozick 1992.
4. See Carter 1990 for the history of agriculture among First Nations peoples.
5. The Saskatchewan land bank has still not had the thorough study it deserves. One view which is widely held is that the land bank was too popular. When land became available, there were thirty applicants but only one could be successful. This had the effect of generating opposition among unsuccessful applicants. See Gidluck (unpublished mss.) and Benson 1991 (unpublished mss.) .

EPILOGUE

The Parable of the Fences

There once was a village named Tomorrow, in a country called Next Year. This village was poor but not destitute. The people were not rich but they had never known famine either. The source of their security was the large herd of cattle they owned.

The road into the village was bounded by fences on both sides. Behind these fences, the cattle were kept. One day a visitor came from the rich nation to the south. He was the mayor of his village and he had come as part of a government-sponsored program to build trading links between the two nations. He observed the fences and said:

> In my country we are very rich. In my country, we let the cattle run free. Cattle that run free have better tasting meat and it is also a more efficient use of the grassland.

The local mayor heard these comments and at the end of the visit declared that from now on all the fences were to be taken down so that they too could become rich. The old people in the village murmured against this innovation but they could not openly oppose their own mayor. One by one the fences were taken down and the people waited for the cattle to roam so they they could become rich.

When ten year old Justice was trampled to death by a charging bull, the children were called together and warned about playing outside. "Justice was a silly boy," they were told, and they each promised not to be so foolish. When Mercy was crushed against the village well during a stampede, the young women were called together and reprimanded for being so careless as to draw water during the daytime. "Mercy was a silly girl," they all agreed, and from then on they only drew water at night.

One hot and humid evening, when the women were all down at the well, word came that the mayor and all his family had been killed when the cattle pushed over the shed where they had gone to sleep. "That was a very silly place to sleep," said Progress. "He should have known better." The women all nodded, each in her turn.

Finally, after a long silence, the old widow Wisdom cleared her throat. "We should all have known better," she said. "Ever since we took down the fences the cattle have had more freedom and we have had less. Now we spend the heat of the day indoors tending children, and labour at night when it is hard to see our work. While we all wait to become rich, we all grow more tired and cry more tears."

"What do you mean," called out Progress boldly. "It is not our fault these people have died. The mayor who visited us said that his nation was rich and his cattle ran free!" The old widow Wisdom slowly turned so that she could address Progress directly. "When I was a child," she said, "I lived in that very village you speak of. It is indeed a rich village but only for some. The mayor has a large family and they are very rich. They live in a walled compound that cannot be damaged by the cattle. The work at the well and in the fields is done by labourers brought from other countries that are not as rich as our neighbours to the south. If they are trampled by the cattle it is of little consequence. There are always more to replace them." The crowd of women stood very still. Even Progress was silent in the face of Wisdom.

When they returned to the village the story was repeated. The next day, everyone in the village set about rebuilding the fences and making the roads safe for the people. The village never became rich, but the time of sadness was past. In honour of the widow, the new enclosures were named after her. To this day they are called the "fences of wisdom."

REFERENCES

Allen, Richard. *The Social Passion: Religion and Social Reform in Canada 1914-1928*. Toronto: University of Toronto Press, 1972.

Allen, Richard, ed. *The Social Gospel in Canada*. Ottawa: National Museum of Man, 1975.

Barber, Benjamin. *Strong Democracy: Participatory Politics for a New Age*. Berkeley: University of California Press, 1984.

Baum, Gregory. *Compassion and Solidarity*. Massey Lecture, Toronto: CBC Enterprises, 1987.

Baum, Gregory. *The Priority of Labour*. New York: Paulist Press, 1982.

Baum, Gregory. "The Shift in Catholic Social Teaching." In *Ethics and Economics*. Edited by Gregory Baum and Cameron. Toronto: Lorimer, 1984.

Bendel, Jake et al. "Saskatchewan Land Cooperative: A Proposal by the International Agricultural Network." April, 1992.

Benson, Marjorie. "Land Bank." Unpublished mss., December 1991.

Berry, Wendell. *Home Economics*. San Francisco: North Point Press, 1987.

Blaug, Mark. *The Methodology of Economics*. Cambridge: Cambridge University Press, 1980: 136-139.

Bobbio, Norberto. "Gramsci and the Conception of Civil Society." In *Gramsci and Marxist Theory*. Edited by Chantal Mouffe. London: Routledge & Kegan Paul, 1979.

Bolton, Sir George. "Background and Emergence of the Eurodollar Market." In *The Eurodollar*. Edited by Herbert V. Prochnow. Chicago: Rand McNally 1970.

Brown, William J., Richard S. Gray, and Pauline J. Molder. "Community Land Trust Models for Saskatchewan." Interchurch Committee on Agriculture, February, 1992.

Callicott, J. Baird. "The Conceptual Foundations of the Land Ethic." In *Companion to A Sand County Almanac*. Edited by J. Baird Callicott. Madison: University of Wisconsin Press, 1987.

Canada, Economic Council of. *A New Frontier: Globalization and Canada's Financial Markets*. Ottawa, 1989.

Canada, Government of. "Survey of the Canadian Foreign Exchange Market." *Bank of Canada Review*. October 1992: 23-35.

Carter, Sarah. *Lost Harvests: Prairie Indian Reserve Farmers & Government Policy*. Montreal: McGill Queen's, 1990.

Charlesworth and Randall, "Morals Markets and the English Crowd in 1766." *Past and Present,* 114 (1987), pp. 206-9.

Christensen, Torben. *Origin and History of Christian Socialism 1848-54*. Copenhagen: Universitetsforlaget, 1962.

Cook, Scott. "The Obsolete 'Anti-Market' Mentality: A Critique of the Substantive Approach to Economic Anthropology." *American Anthropologist,* 68 (1966).

Dalton, George, ed. *Primitive, Archaic Modern Economies: Essays of Karl Polanyi*. Garden City, N.J.: Anchor Books, 1968.

Dearborn, Jeffrey. *How To Prevent Pesticide Pollution*. Beaverton, Oregon: DHJKL Publishing Co., 1991.

Diamond, Barbara B. and Mark P. Kollar. *24-Hour Trading: The Global Network of Futures and Options Markets*. New York: John Wiley & Sons, 1989.

Dorr, Donal. *Option for the Poor: One Hundred Years of Vatican Social Teaching*. Maryknoll, N.Y.: Orbis Books, 1983.

Federal Task Force on Agriculture. *Canadian Agriculture in the Seventies*. Ottawa, 1969.

Fiorenza, Elizabeth Schüssler. "Discipleship and Patriarchy: Early Christian Ethos and Christian Ethics in a Feminist Theological Perspective." In *Women's Consciousness, Women's Conscience: A Reader in Feminist Ethics*. Edited by Barbara Hilkert Andolsen, Christine E. Gudorf and Mary D. Pellauer. Minneapolis: Winston Press, 1985.

Fisher, Elizabeth. *Woman's Creation: Sexual Evolution and the Shaping of Society*. Garden City, N.Y.: Doubleday, 1979.

Frieden, Jeffery A. *Banking On The World: The Politics of American International Finance*. New York: Harper & Row, 1987.

Funabashi, Yoichi. *Managing The Dollar: From the Plaza to the Louvre*. Revised edition. Washington, D.C.: Institute for International Economics, 1989.

George, Susan. *The Debt Boomerang*. London: Pluto Press & Boulder, Colorado: Westview Press, 1992.

Gidluck, Lyn. "The N.D.P. and the Land Bank." Unpublished mss., 1991.

Gilligan, Carol. *In a Different Voice*. Cambridge: Harvard University Press, 1982.

Griffiths, Brian. *The Creation of Wealth*. London: Hodder Stoughton, 1984.

Hamilton, Adrian. *The Financial Revolution*. New York: Viking Penguin, 1986.

Heilbroner, Robert L. "Economics As A 'Value-Free' Science." *Social Research,* 400 (1973): 129-143.

Heim, S. Mark. "Mapping Globalization for Theological Education." In *Theological Education*, Supplement I, 1990: 7-34.

Heyward, Carter. *Our Passion for Justice*. New York: Pilgrim Press, 1984.

Heyward, Carter. *The Redemption of God: A Theology of Mutual Relation*. Washington, D.C.: University Press of America, 1982.

Hill, Stuart B. "Ecological and Psychological Prerequisites for the Establishment of Sustainable Prairie Agricultural Communities." In *Alternative Futures For Prairie Agricultural Communities*. Edited by Jerome Martin. Edmonton:

References

University of Alberta Department of Extension, 1991.

Hillery, G. "Definitions of Community: Areas of Agreement." *Rural Sociology*, 20 (1955).

Hutchinson, T.W. *'Positive' Economics and Policy Judgements*. London: George Allen Unwin, 1964, p. 38.

James, Edwin O. *The Cult of the Mother-Goddess: An Archaeological and Documentary Study*. London: Thames & Hudson, 1959.

Jones, Peter d'A. *The Christian Socialist Revival 1877-1914*. Princeton: Princeton University Press, 1968.

King, A. and B. Schneider. *The First Global Revolution: A Report by the Council of the Club of Rome*. New York: Pantheon Books, 1991.

Kirkpatrick, Frank G. *Community: A Trinity of Models*. Washington: Georgetown University Press, 1986.

Kreiger, Andrew J. *The Money Bazaar: Inside the Trillion-dollar World of Currency Trading*. New York: Times Books, 1992.

Kuttner, Robert. *The End of Laissez-Faire: Global Economy and National Purpose after the Cold War*. New York: Alfred A. Knopf, 1991.

Lebacqz, Karen. "Love Your Enemy: Sex, Power, and Christian Ethics." In *The Annual of the Society for Christian Ethics* 1990. (Distributed by Georgetown University Press, Washington D.C.)

Leiper, Henry Smith. *World Chaos or World Christianity*. Chicago: Willett, Clark & Co., 1937.

Leopold, Aldo. *A Sand County Almanac*. Enlarged edition. New York: Oxford University Press, 1966.

Lerner, Gerda. *The Creation of Patriarchy*. New York: Oxford University Press, 1986.

Levich, Richard and Ingo Walter. "The Regulation of Global Financial Markets." In Noyelle 1989.

Lewis, Michael. *Liar's Poker*. New York: Viking Penguin, 1989.

Lind, Christopher. "Ethics, Economics and Canada's Catholic Bishops." *Canadian Journal of Political and Social Theory,* Fall 1983.

Lind, Christopher. "How Karl Polanyi's Moral Economy Can Help Religious and Other Social Critics." Presented to the Third International Karl Polanyi Conference, Milan, Italy, October 1990.

Lind, Christopher. "The Role of the Churches in the Farm Crisis." PMC: The Practice of Ministry in Canada, November 1992.

Lipietz, Alain. *Mirages and Miracles: The Crises of Global Fordism*. Translated by David Macey. London: Verso, 1987.

Macmurray, John. *Freedom In The Modern World*. London: Faber & Faber, 1932. Reprinted in 1968.

Macmurray, John. *Interpreting the Universe*. London: Faber & Faber, 1936.

Macmurray, John. *Persons In Relation*. London: Faber & Faber, 1961.

Macmurray, John. *The Self As Agent*. London: Faber & Faber, 1956.

McIver, R.M. *Community*. London: Macmillan, 1924.

Moore, Allison Mauel. "Moral Agency of Women in a Battered Women's Shelter." In *The Annual of the Society for Christian Ethics* 1990. (Distributed by Georgetown University Press, Washington D.C.)

Myrdal, Gunnar. *Objectivity in Social Research.* New York: Pantheon, 1969.

Noyelle, Theirry. *New York's Financial Markets: The Challenges of Globalization.* Boulder, Colorado: Westview Press, 1989.

Nozick, Marcia. *No Place Like Home: Building Sustainable Communities.* Ottawa: Canadian Council on Social Development, 1992.

O'Brien, David J. and Thomas A. Shannon, eds. *Renewing the Earth: Catholic Documents on Peace, Justice and Liberation.* New York: Doubleday, 1977.

Ohmae, Kenichi. *The Borderless World.* New York: Harper Business, 1990.

Pearson, Harry, ed. *Livelihood of Man.* New York: Academic Press, 1977.

Polanyi, Karl. *The Great Transformation.* Boston: Beacon Press, 1944. Reprinted in 1957.

Polanyi, Karl. *Karl Polanyi: Essays in Economic Anthropology.* Seattle: American Ethnological Society, 1965.

Polanyi, Karl. "Our Obsolete Market Mentality." *Commentary,* 3, 3 (1947).

Polanyi, Karl et al. *Trade and Market In The Early Empires.* Chicago: Gateway Edition, 1971 [1957].

Porter, Michael. *The Competitive Advantage of Nations.* New York: The Free Press, 1990.

Randall, A. J. (pp29-51) in John Rule ed. *British Trade Unionism 1750-1850.* London: Longman, 1988.

Revised English Bible. Oxford University Press & Cambridge University Press, 1989.

Roberts, Hayden. *Community Development.* Toronto: University of Toronto Press, 1979.

Robinson, Joan. *Economic Philosophy.* Chicago: Aldine, 1963.

Ross, David and Peter Usher. *From the Roots Up: Economic Development as if Community Mattered.* Toronto: James Lorimer Co., 1986.

Rotstein, Abraham. "The Reality of Society: Karl Polanyi's Philosophical Perspective." Paper presented to the Karl Polanyi Commemorative Conference, Hungarian Academy of Sciences, Budapest, October 1986.

Rotstein, Abraham. *Rebuilding from Within: Remedies for Canada's Ailing Economy.* Ottawa: Canadian Institute for Economic Policy, 1984.

Rowe, Stan. *Home Place: Essays on Ecology.* Edmonton: NeWest Publishers, 1990.

Sandel, Michael. *Liberalism and the Limits of Justice.* Cambridge: Cambridge University Press, 1982.

Scott, R.B.Y. and Gregory Vlastos, eds. *Towards the Christian Revolution.* Kingston: Ronald P. Frye, 1989 [1936].

Scruton, Roger. *A Dictionary of Political Thought.* London: Pan Books, [1982] 1983.

Selznick, Philip. *The Moral Commonwealth: Social Theory and the Promise of Community.* Berkeley: University of California Press, 1992.

Sheridan SJ, E.F., ed. *Do Justice! The Social Teaching of the Canadian Catholic*

References

Bishops. Sherbrooke, Quebec: Editions Paulines, 1987.

Sparrow, Hon. Herbert O. et al. *Soil At Risk: Canada's Eroding Future. A Report on Soil Conservation by the Standing Committee on Agriculture, Fisheries, and Forestry, to the Senate of Canada*. Ottawa,1984.

Stewart, John and Holm Tiessen. "Grasslands into Deserts?" In *Planet Under Stress: The Challenge of Global Change*. Edited by Constance Mungall and Digby J. McLaren for the Royal Society of Canada. Toronto: Oxford University Press, 1990.

Strange, Susan. *Casino Capitalism*. Oxford: Basil Blackwell, 1988.

Tawney , R.H. *The Acquisitive Society*. London: Collins, 1921. Reprinted in 1961.

Tawney, R.H. *Religion and the Rise of Capitalism*. Harmondsworth: Penguin, 1938 [1926].

Thomas, Norman E. "From Missions to Globalization: Teaching Missiology in North American Seminaries." *International Bulletin of Missionary Research*, 13 (1989):103-107.

Thompson, E.P. *Customs in Common*. New York: The New Press, 1991.

Thompson, E.P. *The Making of the English Working Class*. London: Victor Gollancz, 1965.

Thompson, E.P. "The Moral Economy of the English Crowd." In Thompson. 1991.

Timmerman, Peter. "Grounds for Concern: Environmental Ethics in the Face of Global Change." In Stewart and Tiessen 1990: 215.

Tœnnies, Ferdinand. *Community and Society (Gemeinschaft und Gesellschaft)*. Translated and edited by Charles P. Loomis. East Lansing: Michigan State University Press, 1957.

Wells, Harold and Roger Hutchinson, eds. *A Long and Faithful March*. Toronto: United Church Publishing House, 1989.

World Resources Institute. *World Resources 1992-93: A Report by the World Resources Institute in Collaboration with the United Nations Environment Programme and the United Nations Development Programme*. New York: Oxford University Press, 1992.

About the Author

Christopher Lind has served as Professor of Church and Society at St. Andrew's College, Saskatoon since 1985. He received his Bachelor of Arts in Political Science from York University, his Master of Divinity from Trinity College and his Ph.D. in Theology specializing in Ethics and Economics from the University of St. Michael's College in Toronto. He has published widely in the areas of ethics and economics, social ethics, Canadian theology and the work of the Canadian Churches in social justice. Other books include *Coalitions for Justice* (Ottawa: Novalis, 1994) edited with Joe Mihevic; and *Justice as Mission: An Agenda for the Church* (Burlington: Trinity Press, 1985) edited with Terry Brown.